The Irish Gardener's Handbook

How to Grow Vegetables, Herbs, Fruit

'Crammed with good organic advice, set out in a simple, readable format' *Irish Garden*

'A practical paperback aimed at those growing their own food on this island' *The Irish Times Magazine*

'Specifically attuned to the Irish climate, which can differ in crucial ways when it comes to growing fruit and vegetables' *Books Ireland*

'Packed with excellent down-to-earth advice and cultural techniques clearly based on years of experience' *Irish Examiner*

'A very handy little Irish publication, a no-frills paperback for those interested in growing their own food' *Image Interiors*

MICHAEL BRENOCK grew up in Mitchelstown, County Cork, in a market-gardening family. He later studied horticulture, and worked on various local authority schemes designed to encourage home-gardening and self-sufficiency, until the demise of such schemes in the 1970s. He also worked at Teagasc, helping to develop commercial vegetable growing. He always kept his own garden and supplied his family with fresh, organic fruit and vegetables, combining the old ways with a scientific background and modern techniques. He was one of the expert panel members on Jerry Daly's RTE radio programme 'Ask about Gardening' from its beginning, and also on the previous series of 'Ask about Gardening' presented by Des Kenny and, even earlier, by John Fanning. He contributed to those programmes on a regular basis for about twenty years. While working as an advisor with Cork County Committee of Agriculture, he gave a regular topical talk on a gardening subject on RTE Radio, Cork.

THE IRISH GARDENER'S HANDBOOK

HOW TO GROW
VEGETABLES, HERBS, FRUIT

Michael Brenock

THE O'BRIEN PRESS
DUBLIN

First published 2010 by The O'Brien Press Ltd,
12 Terenure Road East, Rathgar, Dublin 6, D06 HD27, Ireland.
Tel: +353 1 4923333; Fax: +353 1 4922777
E-mail: books@obrien.ie
Website: www.obrien.ie
Reprinted 2010, 2014, 2019, 2021.
The O'Brien Press is a member of Publishing Ireland.

ISBN: 978-1-84717-193-1

8 7 6 5
23 22 21

Cover photographs courtesy of iStockphoto.

Printed and bound by CPI Group (UK) Ltd, Croydon, CR0 4YY
The paper in this book is produced using pulp from managed forests.

Published in:

DUBLIN
UNESCO
City of Literature

Acknowledgements

From the time my late father put a tomato seedling into my hands when I was six years of age, I was hooked on gardening. I grew up absorbing garden lore, which became horticultural science in UCD. I would like to thank Dr Owen Goodman, who was an unsung mentor and inspirational teacher in Johnstown Castle, Wexford, then a residential horticultural college.

I always felt that I needed to put my thoughts and ideas in print and share the joys of gardening. This book is the culmination of that effort. I wish to thank Darina Allen, not only for her preface, but for guiding me in the right direction to Ide ní Laoghaire. Ide is an inspiration and has a wonderful capacity to absorb the material and turn it into a more presentable form.

I have to say thanks to so many. First of all to my wife, Ruth, who encouraged me and nearly developed an interest in gardening herself! To my family, who avidly followed the progress of the book – who never appreciated good, fresh, home-grown vegetables as children, but are now my biggest fans. My two grandsons, Oisin and Niall, who are natural-born gardeners and already connoisseurs of tomatoes and soft fruits, organic of course, and my two grand-daughters, Sophie and Aisling, who are more interested in flower gardening – but they will learn!

My sincere thanks to Marguerite Fleming and Bernie Flynn, both keen gardeners, for reading the first draft of the book and for their constructive comments. To my former colleagues in Teagasc: Gerry Walsh, Gorey; Stephen Alexander, Dublin; Andrew Whelton, Cork; and Paddy Hanrahan, Bantry, for their suggestions and tips. To Michael Cregan, who kept the pressure on me to get it finished.

I wish to thank the very many people I met over my career as an advisor in horticulture, who encouraged me to write this, who asked me questions and who offered me solutions to problems. I hope that this book answers all those questions and that gardening will continue to provide so much pleasure to all of you.

Contents

HOW TO GROW, CROP BY CROP

VEGETABLES

HERBS

FRUIT

Soft Fruits

Tree fruits

THINGS YOU MAY NEED TO KNOW

INTRODUCTION

Darina Allen

In the early seventies, when I was newly married and hugely enjoying playing house for the first time, I fantasised about having my own little vegetable and herb garden close to the kitchen, like we'd had at home. My mother and grandmother were both keen gardeners, so I had learned a little from them. But I was anxious to learn more, so I enrolled in a series of gardening classes at the Midleton vocational school.

As luck would have it, Michael was teaching the classes. Even at that stage he had a passion to pass on his skills – skills garnered from his childhood home, then from his scientific training in horticulture. However, I pestered him about organic growing! I'm not sure he saw the merit of this initially, steeped as he was in science, but he certainly does now. Few people have the depth of knowledge that Michael has. Even as a child, he helped to sow seeds and plant seedlings in his father's market garden, then expanded his knowledge as an adult home gardener and horticultural instructor. He currently spends a lot of time as an allotment advisor, helping people grow their own.

Several times during the past twenty years, Michael mentioned to me that he would like to write a book, putting his knowledge on a more permanent footing and making it available to a wider audience. Recently, with the demise of the Celtic Tiger, the need became more urgent. A growing number of people now see the value of self-sufficiency – and not just for economic reasons, but also for the sheer joy and satisfaction of growing your own vegetables. In a sudden flash of inspiration, I introduced Michael to Íde ní Laoghaire of the O'Brien Press, who was quick to see the potential.

I think this has resulted in a brilliantly useful book, with a clear layout, which makes it easy – even for complete beginners – to access the information they need to give them the confidence to start growing, even if their first efforts are in a window box or a teapot on a balcony! And even for old hands, Michael's encyclopaedic knowledge will add to their experience, and result in a bountiful kitchen garden.

I am proud to be associated with this timely tome, which is bound to enhance the lives of many.

Preface

This book is aimed at home gardeners, allotment growers, and would-be gardeners in Ireland. The Irish climate and soils make particular demands on us gardeners, and we Irish also have our own approach and attitude to soils and crops. We like to eat certain things, we like to grow certain things – most Irish people, for example, just love to grow their own potatoes. These traditions are important. Up to a generation or two ago, we were largely an agricultural people with our roots firmly in the earth. Things have moved on and now there is very little home production of fruit and vegetables – but this is changing and vegetable gardening is fast becoming a new, even fashionable, interest. Fortunately, this is happening when we still have people in our communities who remember the old ways – people like me! We can pass on the information about food production on a small scale as carried on by our forebears in our own very wilful climate, and most of us have also kept up with more recent trends in gardening, such as the great interest in raised beds, as well as carrying on the old ways and keeping forgotten skills alive.

There are huge variations in climate in Ireland, even within short distances, and there are millions of very local micro climates – we need to understand how to deal with these. We have many different soil types because of the geological variations – these provide opportunities as well as challenging us to get the best out of them. We have a wonderful opportunity to explore and exploit these factors in our own gardens or in an allotment near us. Even if the weather exasperates us at times, it's most important to remember that Ireland is a very good place for gardening. Crops grow well here. In the recent past, many people fed their families largely by their own efforts. Nowadays, many wish to do the same, and become at least partly self-sufficient. How best to manage that is our business in this book.

I hope this book will be helpful to anybody who has never grown vegetables or herbs or fruit, but who is thinking of doing so. I hope it will also be encouraging to those who have tried, and, for one reason or another, have given up, perhaps because of bad weather, other commitments, bad advice or pure lack of know-how. Many people have started growing their own because they like to know exactly what they are eating, others like to have their vegetables and fruit really fresh. Very few do it because it is cheaper – though it is. Freshness, flavour and absence of chemicals are the chief motives for people growing their own, and in my opinion they are worthy motives.

People have become more health conscious. We like our vegetables fresh, we relish good flavour and are conscious of how far our food has travelled. There is a wonderful display of fresh vegetables and fruit in our supermarkets, and this produce looks clean and attractive. Of course, these foods must comply with the rules laid down by the food safety authorities that residue levels of chemicals allowed are under a certain maximum. But if people had a choice, most would opt for a chemical-free product. Growing your own gives you complete control over what is used to grow the crops. Chemicals, whether fertilisers, fungicides, insecticides or herbicides are all aids to crop production and without them it would be impossible to produce products in the supermarkets in the quantity, quality, variety and at the low prices that pertain at present. Many people, however, are gladly opting to buy natural, organic produce, though it is more expensive.

By growing your own, whether in your own garden or in an allotment, you have control over what goes into your favourite fruit or vegetables. You will benefit from the freshness and flavour of your own produce, the convenience and choice. You will benefit from the physical exercise involved in its production, and don't underestimate the therapeutic value of working with nature and watching crops develop under your management. There will be days, and sometimes many days, when you will be unable to work in the garden, but this will simply whet your appetite all the more when conditions are right.

Michael Brenock

Getting Started

So, you've decided to grow you own veg. Great! Here are the basics things you need to get started:

- **Equipment**: spade (long-handled), fork (long-handled), shovel, boots, rake, hoe, watering can, trowel; gardening gloves are nice, but not essential. Later, a wheelbarrow is really handy (in an allotment you might share this with others).
- **What should I grow?** This depends on your family's tastes. Start with the things you like to eat. You can always experiment in future years. The crops are listed in the HOW TO GROW section according to 'permanent' or 'annual', then herbs, soft fruits, tree fruits – in alphabetical order. Flick through this and select what you would like to grow.
- **What can I grow?** All the crops in the HOW TO GROW section are marked EASY, DIFFICULT etc. Select the ones you feel you can manage. If you are a real beginner, it may be best to stick with those marked EASY – but it's great to try something gardeners generally regard as difficult and get good results. Having fun is important too!
- **The result?** Chemical-free vegetables and fruits, absolutely fresh produce for your table, chemical-free herbs within easy, immediate reach, a degree of self-sufficiency that is very satisfying.

(More details on gardening issues and practices are given in the 'Things You May Need to Know' section, page 248. That section may help you improve your site and your gardening habits, and it allows you to check up on such issues where necessary.)

Headings Used for Instructions
– what they mean

HOW TO GROW

The specific growing instructions for each crop are covered. (Not all plants fit into the exact same plan, so occasional extra headings are used where appropriate.)

Seeds

Seeds can often be planted either indoors or outdoors. Times are given for both where appropriate.

EARLIEST, LATEST AND BEST SOWING DATES:

Earliest time to sow: is the earliest date, consistent with soil and air temperatures, in which the seeds will germinate satisfactorily and the plants will be ready to grow on where they are sown or transplanted out after hardening-off. The earliest-sown crop usually gives the earliest harvest, but not always the best, and often suffers from more pests and diseases and uneven growth.

Latest time to sow: is the date by which the seed should be sown to complete its life cycle and produce a satisfactory crop. Sowing later than that date may give a smaller, immature crop or one that does not store properly.

Best time to sow: the date that past experience has shown to give the most consistent good returns, when soil and weather conditions are more amenable to plant growth and development. The best date may also consider the prevalence of pests at that time.

Depth of sowing: the depth at which seeds are sown is largely determined by the size of the seed. The bigger the seed, the greater the depth of sowing. Sowing too deeply may lead to seed rotting or slow and erratic germination, while too shallow sowing may lead to non-germination or drying out during germination, causing the death of the seed.

Germination time: this is the normal time that it takes a seed to germinate at the recommended temperature.

Lifespan of seeds: this is the normal viable life of seeds from the time they are produced on the parent plant until they fail to germinate under normal conditions.

Successional sowings: this tells you when to make follow-up sowings after the first one to give continuity of cropping.

Plants

Most crops are grown outdoors. Some are sown outdoors as seed, and others are sown indoors and transplanted outside. Transplanting refers to those plants that are raised inside in trays, pots or cells, and hardened-off, or raised outside in seedbeds. If you buy plants rather than sowing seed, you follow the instructions for planting outdoors.

Earliest time to plant: this refers to the soil and air temperatures that are suitable for plants to be planted outside. Plants raised inside for growing outside need to be hardened-off or acclimatised to the normal outdoor weather conditions.

Latest time to plant: this refers to the time after which a plant may not reach full maturity because of shortening days.

Stage of growth: this means the stage of growth of the plant when it is best for transplanting. Plants being planted or transplanted outside are usually at the third or fourth rough-leaf stage (see p30).

Best aspect: aspect refers to the direction that the garden slopes, and in Ireland the best aspect is southerly.

Best soil: some crops prefer light, sandy soils, while others like medium loams. The soil can be improved in texture or enriched by adding manure or compost.

Soil preparation: the preparation of soil begins a long time before sowing or planting; includes digging, improving the texture and adding manures or compost where appropriate.

Space between plants: this is the minimum distance between plants to allow for full development to take place. Consideration is given for development of roots and the access of leaves to sunlight.

Distance between rows: this is the minimum distance for walking between rows or for using a hoe between rows, or for earthing-up.

Occasional headings, used where relevant:

Best position: the most suitable position in the garden, considering aspect, shelter and soil.

Distance between seeds: when seeds are sown in a line for thinning-out later, eg carrots, they are sown thinly – less than 1cm (½in) apart. When thinned-out, plants are spaced 4–5cm (1.5–2in) apart. The thicker the seeds were sown, the more you need to remove and discard, and this is wasteful of seed.

Distance between rows of seeds: the minimum distance between adjacent rows of either the same vegetables or other vegetables. This distance allows ample space for development of the crop, both roots and leaves, and also allows for weeding and hoeing between rows.

Germination temperature: the best temperature for germination.

Sowing in cells for transplanting: seeds may be sown in pots or cells for transplanting out later, after hardening-off. This is distinct from sowing them in a seed tray or a seedbed or in rows inside or outside.

Best time to plant: the optimal time to plant plants, considering soil conditions, weather, growth stage of plant and when it's most likely to escape attacks of pests and diseases. The best time to get the best yields.

Depth of planting: the depth to which a plant should be put into the soil, usually to the soil mark on the stem of the plant.

How to plant: instructions on how particular plants are planted, including trees, bushes and young vegetable plants. Includes depth and size of hole, depth of stem in the hole, filling and packing, staking.

Thinning-out: picking out surplus plants in a row of young seedlings, usually at second to third rough-leaf stage. The spacing between plants will vary for different crops: carrots as close as 4–5cm (2in); swedes 12–15cm (5–6in). Thinnings of some crops can be transplanted, eg lettuce, while turnips and swedes cannot. Always water the crop before thinning and again afterwards.

Propagation of celery (and celeriac): celery is difficult to propagate from seed and has a light requirement as well as a temperature requirement of 65°F (18.5°C) before germination takes place and for 2–3 weeks after seedlings emerge.

Average or expected yield per plant: the average yield from a plant or bush when fully mature; this is given where relevant.

Lifespan: the length of life of a tree or plant that is well cared for by pruning, manuring, and by pest, disease and weed control.

How to harvest: instructions are given where there is a special method of harvesting.

Disposal of plants: after the crop has been harvested from a plant the remains of the plant are pulled up and put on the compost heap.

Number of plants needed for good yield: this is obviously a matter of taste and how many of a particular vegetable or fruit you want to have; many plants provide one fruit per plant, eg one head of lettuce per lettuce plant, so it's easy to estimate how many you will need. In some cases, where it is not quite so obvious (eg brussels sprouts), I give the approximate number of plants required to gave an average family a supply of that vegetable or fruit when in season.

Staking: required in the case of peas and scarlet runner beans. Instead of stakes or bamboo canes, netting or a mesh of wire or plastic supported by stakes and wire may be used and should be put in place at time of planting or before.

Stages of Growing

1 SEEDS

SOWING SEEDS

- Seed comes in sealed packets, usually with sufficient seed to supply the average needs of a household.

- Seed can be got at garden centres, your local garden supply shop and some general shops or supermarkets, and from a number of mail-order seed firms (see Appendix). Many of these stock organic seed. Increasingly, because of cost, people are saving their own seed, keeping it from year to year – and also swapping seeds as they did long ago.

- The seed packet usually has a lot of information on it about the sowing of the seed, including the 'sow by' date. This is usually very accurate and concise. But remember, the instructions are usually for the British situation, and that is sometimes a full month ahead of Irish conditions in terms of the soil warming up.

- **Pelleted seed**: small seed is sometimes coated with inert clay so as to form a pellet for ease of sowing. These seeds are usually more short-lived than untreated seeds as the moistening process involved in pelleting usually starts off the germination process temporarily.

- **Taped seed**: individual seeds are put in between two rolls of tape at specific spaces, and the tape is laid along a shallow furrow and covered with soil. The tape is water soluble, and as soon as the tape dissolves, the seed absorbs moisture, and germination starts.

Where to sow

- Seeds are sown indoors and/or outdoors depending on the crop, the time of year and on your choice of site.

  Outdoors:

- **Direct sowing /direct drilling**: sow the seeds directly into the ground where they are to mature at a later date. Thinning-out may be required.

- **Sow in seedbed**: seed is sown in rows or scattered into a specially prepared seedbed to be lifted and transplanted to a new location later on, where they are to grow and mature.

- **Seedbeds**: specially-prepared small areas of ground where seeds are sown; they are located in a favoured spot in the garden (warm and sheltered), where pests can be prevented or controlled easily. It is easier than preparing a larger area and keeping it free of pests, diseases and weeds. Plants are selected to be transplanted from here to somewhere else in the garden.

- *Indoors*:

- **Sowing under protection**: usually done under glass or in a polythene tunnel, with or without heat, usually in seed trays or pots to be hardened-off as the plants grow before planting outside.

How to sow

- **Sowing singly**: where seeds are large enough to be handled individually, for example courgettes or broad beans, they can be sown individually into the soil or into flower pots or cellular trays (trays that may have 6–12 or more individual pots or cells united together).

- **Broadcast**: finer seeds may be scattered at random over a definite area of ground to be covered with a layer of soil – in a seed tray or in a seedbed outdoors, or under glass or plastic.

- **Sowing thinly**: seeds are sown as thinly as possible; but sow more than you need to allow for loss to pests, diseases and bad seed.

- Pour the seed from the packet into the palm of the hand or into a saucer or some such container.

- Pinch the seed between the thumb and forefinger, a few at a time, and spread them very thinly into a narrow line in the ground.

- Never feel that all the seed must be sown at once.

- Put a marker or label at the end of the row or drill at sowing time, not the following day, and note it in your notebook or diary if you are keeping one.

- The soil should be firm enough that it can be walked on without leaving deep footprints. It should be soft enough to be able to press a finger into the soil and hard enough to avoid air pockets. As a seed germinates, the emerging root must be able to get a root-hold and also be able to get air. The seedbed should be cultivated only when soil conditions are dry and not sticky.

Germination

- For germination to take place it is necessary to have heat, air and moisture. There is a minimum temperature to be reached before germination can occur and this varies from species to species.

- Large seeds, like peas, beans, beetroot and chard may be soaked in water overnight before sowing and this speeds up the process.

- Temperature for germination varies with each crop. The minimum temperature will get some of them off, but the optimum temperature will see the majority germinate. Check the packet for temperature guide. The minimum temperature for most vegetable seeds is around 7°C (45°F).

- **Germination time**: this varies for each kind of vegetable; for example, turnips germinate in a few days depending on weather, whereas parsnips could take a month. Temperature influences the time span of germination.

- **Depth of sowing**: the depth of sowing will depend on the size of the seed. The covering depth is the same as the diameter of the seed (at its greatest dimension). It is the depth of the compost when pressed that matters.

- **Viability of seeds**: the viability of seeds is the number of years they will last and still germinate. Many people buy seeds and the information is given on the packet, usually a 'sow-by date' or a date of packaging. However, many people are now germinating their own seeds, so it's important to know the lifespan. Some seeds have a naturally long lifespan, for example turnips, while parsnip seeds have a short life. This viability is influenced by the storage conditions of the seed, especially temperature and moisture – seed is expensive, so do store it properly in cool, dry conditions, in an airtight jar. Seed is a living thing and must be treated as such.

- **Germination test**: seed can be tested for germination by counting out 100 seeds and placing them on damp blotting paper or sand, and placing in a warm place. Keep moist and count out the numbers that germinate and this gives the percentage germination. The numbers should be in the high eighties; discard any seed with less than 50% germination.

- **Seed vigour**: this is an extra test to germination. Even though all the seeds may germinate under near perfect germination conditions, there may be too much of a time lapse between those first emerging and those emerging last. Those emerging last usually lack vigour and will be slow or fail to emerge if not in ideal conditions and this backwardness will be reflected in poor growth and small size of the plant eventuality. Old seed that is no longer viable should be put on the compost heap.

- **Continuous or successional sowing**: sowing seed at regular intervals to give continuity of cropping. For example, lettuce crops for about three weeks before it gets tough or bolts/goes to seed, and then the next sowing should be ready to begin harvesting. Radishes mature faster and need to be sown at shorter intervals, while carrots need only two sowings in the year, early and main crop, for an average household usage.

- **Best varieties**: varieties of vegetables and fruits have different characteristics and qualities, including earliness or lateness, hardiness, flavour, pest and disease resistance, size, keeping quality, shape and colour. There are other factors, but it is the various combinations of these that make such a great collection of varieties available. Those that I have recommended in this book are the varieties that I know well and have observed over many years. There are many more, but I can stand over my advice on these particular varieties. In my opinion, the most important characteristics are pest and disease resistance, flavour, earliness, keeping quality.

- **F1 Hybrids**: these hybrids are produced by crossing two unrelated purebred hybrids and they produce a very uniform crop, with increased vigour. Their major disadvantage is that all the plants tend to mature at the same time, with no spread. Never save seed from an F1 hybrid as the progeny are totally unpredictable. I would buy an F1 of sweetcorn, onions or tomatoes – any crop that can be stored well – but not of cauliflower or broccoli, crops that do not store well!

- **Open pollinated**: this is seed that is produced from plants that produce blossom and are openly pollinated by wind or insects. This is in contrast to closed pollination or F1 hybrids where two distinct but unrelated varieties of a crop are pollinated by hand and the resulting hybrid is a superior or enhanced type with very desirable characteristics such as disease or pest resistance, earliness, bigger size, better taste, colour or keeping quality.

- **Certified seed potatoes**: these are certified by the Department of Agriculture and are a good way to start growing potatoes. They do not normally carry potato blight, and they are guaranteed to be free of viral diseases and eelworms, both of which are the most debilitating problems in potatoes. Viral diseases can be carried by some varieties and show no symptoms; they spread to healthy stalks in the field and cause severe crop losses. It is a risk to accept seed from sources that were not grown from certified seed in the previous year or two.

- **Beetroot seed**: the 'seed' can produce 2–3 plants, and the seed in this case is really a fruit and not a monogerm (single seed). The fruit contains 2–3 real seeds and this explains how 2–3 plants emerge from the one 'seed' sown.

- **Dangers to seed at germination stage**: *Botrytis,* also called *grey mould* causes damping off in emerging seedlings. If this occurs, avoid watering and anything that dampens the atmosphere. Raise the temperature to reduce humidity.

2 SEEDLINGS TO PLANTS

- **Watering seedlings**: seedlings should be watered before the surface of the compost dries out fully. The seedlings should not be over-watered as this leads to leaching out of nutrients and to a damp atmosphere.

• **Pricking-out/pricking-off**: taking out individual seedlings from a seed tray at the first or second rough-leaf stage and planting each one into open ground, or a pot or cellular tray filled with compost, where it establishes itself as an independent plant. Seedlings are pricked-out at various stages of development, usually at the second or third rough-leaf stage, or as soon as they are fit to handle. The sooner they are planted out the better, as there is less damage to the roots and the seedlings recover faster. Some crops need to be pricked-out early in their development stage, for example celery and tomatoes are best done at the first rough-leaf stage. Cabbages can be left until the second rough-leaf stage. Instructions are given for each crop.

• **Potting-off/potting-up**: taking individual plants from a seed tray or seedbed and putting them into individual pots or cells to grow as independent plants where the roots are completely separated from roots of other plants.

• **Potting-on**: taking plants that are already in pots and re-potting them into a larger-sized pot, usually a size or two larger, for example from 16cm to 18cm.

• **Hardening-off**: this is the process of acclimatising plants from the warm atmosphere of a glasshouse or tunnel to the normal outdoor weather. It is normally done in the spring to early summer period by putting the plants outside for a few hours during a warm, sunny day and taking them in at night. By gradually extending the time outside, the plants become acclimatised to the normal outdoor weather when they can be left outside overnight. On a night that frost is fore-cast, the plants should be either taken inside or given some cover or protection, such as newspapers or black plastic sheeting.

- **Bought-in plants**: those plants that are raised by a plant propagator to be planted in the garden. They are usually already hardened-off, ready for planting. The dangers are that they can carry pests and diseases, or be diseased themselves. They can also carry weeds and seeds of weeds.

- **Thinning-out**: selecting and pulling out the weaker plants, leaving the better plants to grow at a predetermined spacing. Plants should be watered well before thinning takes place as this lessens the damage to the roots as they are being pulled. The plants are thinned to the recommended distance apart and that is given in the instructions for each individual crop.

- **What to do with thinnings**: you can transplant some, such as cabbages and lettuces; leeks and onions may also be transplanted, but with great care. Others are less successful, such as carrots, parsnips, swedes – put on the compost heap.

- **When to transplant or thin-out**: when the plants have reached the second rough-leaf stage (see below). The earlier it is done, the less damage is suffered by the plants remaining.

Development of seedling

- **Seed leaf**: this is the first leaf or leaves that emerge from the seed as it germinates. It is usually simple in shape and differs completely from the true or normal leaf of the crop or vegetable.

- **Rough leaf or true leaf**: the first true leaf, or rough leaf, emerges as the seed leaf begins to die back or turns yellow (botanists refer to them as true leaves, but gardeners, confusingly, call them rough leaves; some plants, eg parsnips, have three leaf stages – seed leaf, first rough leaf, true rough leaf!). The rough leaves develop gradually, in sequence, and are indicative of equal development in the roots. The first rough leaf normally develops within a week of the seedling emerging and the second rough leaf may come 1–3 weeks later, depending on the vegetable.

- **When to transplant**: instructions regarding transplanting usually refer to the second or third rough-leaf stage. These leaves indicate that the plants are big enough to handle and have a good root structure.

3 PLANTING

- **Planting-out**: lifting plants from where they germinated to another location in the garden or polytunnel or glasshouse.
- **Depth of planting**: plants should always be planted to the soil mark on their stem. If planted too deep, the stem will be damaged by the soil, and if planted too shallow, they will easily be blown over and less roots are available to the plant.
- **How to plant**: to transplant plants, use either a trowel, dibber or the fingers to make the hole into which you will place the plants.
- Plants should be firm enough on planting that when a leaf is pulled, the plant remains in the ground and the leaf tears. The soil should be firm enough so that the roots can have good contact with the surrounding soil without any air pockets.
- The plants should be watered immediately, especially in dry weather, and given protection against pests such as pigeons and rabbits, by using nets.
- Put a marker or label at the end of the row or drill, and note it in your notebook or diary.

- **Soil preparation**: many gardeners like to dig the garden over the winter and leave the soil rough and exposed to the frost and rain over the late winter and early spring. I find this good practice.

- The soil should be broken into a friable, crumbly structure, with no lumps left or clods with roots of grass or weeds attached. Large stones over 5cm (2in) in diameter are removed and so also are any roots of perennial weeds, like nettles, thistles, docks, bindweed and scutch grass. For seed-sowing, the soil is raked to a very fine quality, but for plants the bed does not need to be as fine. The bed should be fine enough to allow small roots to penetrate the soil, and firm enough to allow roots to get a grip. Where manure or compost is added, it should be thoroughly mixed with the soil so there are no large accumulations in any one spot that would damage the young, developing roots.

- **Space between plants**: the space to allow between plants depends on the crops. Where drills are used, you can plant them tighter – the wider the drills, the closer plants can go as they will compensate by growing into the space between the drills.

- Adequate spacing allows good circulation of air and this can help in the prevention and control of diseases and pests.

- Adequate spacing makes hoeing and weeding easier.

- The wider the spacing, the bigger the size of root or fruit – carrots will be tiny if only 1cm (½in) apart, but will be very large at 15cm (6in) spacing.

- Very wide spacing delays harvesting dates as the plant has to grow more. The crops will be bigger, but this is not always an advantage.

- **Distance between rows or drills**: the distance between rows allows room to walk, and room for foliage to grow without overcrowding. But too wide a space between rows also gives more space for weeds to grow. Rows of lettuce can be as close as 30cm (12in), onions, beetroot and carrots 45cm (18in), but potatoes and French beans need about 60cm (24in) and peas 120–150cm (4–5ft) between *rows*.

4 MANAGEMENT

- Keep a close look on the plants for the onset of any pest or disease and take prompt control measures. If birds or rabbits are likely to attack, then nets should be put up before any damage is done.
- Water and feed before plants show signs of stress.
- Keep weeds under control and earth-up with soil where necessary.
- **Feeds for vegetables**: organic feeds are made-up mixtures of nettles or comfrey leaves soaked in water for a number of weeks. The solution is drained off and diluted one part to a hundred in water; this is watered into the roots of plants every week. The more diluted the feed is, the easier it is for the plant to take it up – dilute more, feed more often.
- **Earthing-up**: this means putting soil up around plants such as potato stalks, cabbage and cauliflower stems. The soil is put up with either a shovel or drawn up with a hoe, and may be done in one or two operations (at 2–3 week intervals). It is done in potatoes as the stalks emerge to prevent frost damage. The second earthing-up is done when stalks are growing rapidly and the soil is raised up to prevent the developing potatoes becoming exposed to sunlight. The earthing-up in cabbages and cauliflowers is done to stabilise or steady the plant and prevent it being blown around by the wind, as

well as keeping weeds under control.

Pollination: pollination is usually associated with apples, and fruit in general, but pollination is an important part of the production of such crops as peas, beans, sweetcorn, vegetable marrows, cucumbers, pumpkins. Pollen must be transferred from the male flower in the case of vegetable marrows, courgettes, pumpkins, cucumbers; and pollen is transferred from the male part (stamens) to the pistil (female part) in the case of peas, beans and sweetcorn. Normally insects do the pollen transfer, but if the weather is cold and damp it may be necessary to assist in the pollination process.

WATERING

Useful watering and feeding aid for raised beds or containers: use washed, discarded plastic 2–4 litre containers with screwtop lids. Drill a small hole (just big enough for the water to drip or seep out) in the lid. Fill with water or liquid feed, screw on the top and place it upside down beside the plant to be fed or watered. In this way the water goes down to the roots and does not run off the surface. Smaller containers have to be filled more often.

5 PESTS, DISEASES AND DEFICIENCIES

APHIDS

- Aphids, also called greenfly or blackfly, are tiny winged *or* wingless insects that can reproduce sexually as well as asexually and can give rise to living young as well as eggs. They attack virtually all plants and can cause a lot of damage, both direct and indirect, in a short space of time.

- The direct damage is caused by aphids sucking the sap from plants, causing distortion and death.

- The indirect damage is caused by the transmission of viral diseases.

- Many of the species can over-winter as eggs on woody plants and in spring these hatch out to produce winged aphids. But the aphid does not require a woody plant stage to over-winter if climatic conditions are suitable – temperatures at or below freezing point can be tolerated by them for short periods of a few days. These winged aphids fly or are carried by wind to host plants where they lay eggs. The eggs hatch out (usually from 50 to 100) and within a week these can give birth (asexually) to living young at the rate of five per day for up to 30 days; the young, in turn, continue the process, so that inside a few weeks, under favourable conditions, the numbers can literally explode. As the host plant begins to die or is incapable of producing any more sap, a number of winged aphids are produced and these can either sexually or asexually produce another generation in a new host plant.

- The fross or white material extruded by the aphids is rich in sugars and nitrogen; they are thus host to many insects, including lacewings, ladybird beetles and hoverwing larvae. The presence of these parasites indicates the presence of aphids.

- The best control is to keep the host plant under observation and remove all weeds; keep woody host plants like hawthorn or willow away from the garden. Where control measures are to be taken they should be taken as soon as the first aphid is seen. Get rid of plants that have bolted, are damaged or are surplus to requirements.

- **What to look for**: aphids occur and multiply in warm weather especially after a few fine days in a row. Always look for them on the underside of the leaves. If there is only one aphid present, then within a few fine days there will be several hundred!

- **What to do**: washing-up liquid or soft soap (found at garden supply shops) diluted in water are safe and effective for the control of aphids in the early stages of attack. Squirt some of the liquid into a gallon of water, enough to give a foam, stir well and apply with a pressure sprayer directly onto the aphids. Applying with a watering can is not sufficient and the underside of the leaves *must* be sprayed. I have always found this effective, but I have always sprayed before the aphids are present in large numbers. Actually, it is the physical disturbance that gets rid of them; they don't like a wet atmosphere and the soft soap or washing-up liquid adds a stickiness that prevents their movement.

SLUGS

- Slugs are one of the greatest pests the gardener could have and the damage they do by far outdoes any benefits they offer, though they do help reduce plant waste to rotted humus.
- Weather, especially moisture, plays a big part in their activity and though they dislike cold, frosty weather, they can survive in egg form several centimetres deep in the soil to re-emerge in spring when temperatures rise and growth of plants starts.
- They are nocturnal creatures, but in very damp weather they can be active during the day.
- Keep the garden free of weeds and leftover plants lying around – slugs love animal manures, lush growth caused by excess nitrogen or too much liquid feed, poor drainage, excessive mulches on top of soil.
- Their natural predators are frogs, centipedes and black ground beetles. Birds also feed on them and the looser a soil is left by tilling and

hoeing, the easier it will be for the birds to get at them.

Slug baits/traps:

- Many materials will help to slow their progress though not eliminate them. Crushed eggshells, hydrated lime, soot and ashes laid along the ground around a plant, or on the attack route, are a good idea.
- I have tried organic slug pellets, but I find them to be of little use.
- The best control is to be watchful. I have often put out squares of cardboard or newspaper in between plants and a few days later just turned them over and picked off the slugs and put it back down again. I have picked off slugs up to 15cm (6in) long and some as tiny as ½cm (¼in). I put them on the compost heap (where they should be working, breaking down the stuff you want broken down).
- In moist weather, examine plants, especially emerging seedlings, before damage is too severe. Put out traps of jampot covers filled with beer at soil level near plants and the following morning there should be some dead slugs in or near the beer.
- **SNAILS**: these behave exactly the same as slugs, and everything above applies to them as well.

BORON

- Boron is a naturally occurring element in the soil and is necessary for successful plant growth. Some families of plants, especially brassicas (or cabbage and turnip family), are particularly prone to deficiencies of Boron. This shows up in turnips as a physiological upset such as browning or blackening in the centres of turnips and swedes which renders them inedible. To prevent this happening, Borax should be added (this is a Boron compound obtainable at a chemist's shop); one teaspoonful in 20 litres of water is sufficient for 50 square metres (10m x 5m). This should be applied before sowing or planting, and once in the season is sufficient. Solubor, obtainable from some garden centres or agricultural suppliers, is used for the same purpose. This is the one occasion on which I would use a replacement chemical element – Boron already exists in the soil and it is very difficult to restore the correct balance without following the above suggestions.

- **Burgundy Mixture**: I don't use this, but many people spray it on potatoes and some other vegetables to prevent blight. It is composed of 4 parts (by weight) of copper sulphate to 5 parts (by weight) of washing soda – 100gm copper sulphate/125gm washing soda/12.5 litres water. Dissolve the copper sulphate in most of the water; dissolve the washing soda in the rest of the water; add the washing soda solution to the copper sulphate. Apply immediately, using a pressure sprayer. Put on as fine a spray as possible, especially on the undersides of the leaves. You should wear protective clothing and a mask and gloves while spraying; wash hands afterwards.

PROTECTION FROM PESTS

- **Clear plastic mulch**: a sheet of very light clear polythene (same grade as used by dry cleaners) with small holes; put over plants to help exclude pests.
- **Fleece**: comes in various sizes of non-woven material that allows rain and light through, but stops insects. It is used in the same way as clear plastic mulch above. It can be re-used for many years and when used on early carrots it also excludes the carrot-root fly.

6 HARVESTING

- **Continuous harvesting**: linked to successional sowing. Whilst the
ideal is to have a continuous supply of fresh vegetables at the peak
of perfection at all times, this is not easily achieved. Most vegetables
will have a run-in period, when the crop is small and immature but
useable, followed by the bulk of the crop being large and flavoursome. This is followed by the 'tailings' or the late maturers, which
are still useable, but losing flavour and quality. To overcome these
shortcomings, more sowings are made so as to overlap to maintain
quality.

- **Bolting, buttoning, going to seed**: bolting or buttoning is a term
used to indicate that a plant has gone from the vegetative or normal
growth stage to the adult or reproductive stage prematurely. It is
normal for most vegetables to produce seed in their second year, as
most of them are biennials. Factors that tend to encourage bolting are:
too high or too low temperatures, shortage of water or nutrients,
sudden shock from transplanting or sowing too early or failing to
harden-off properly – anything that causes uneven or irregular
growth. The person who raises their own plants from seed has control
over these conditions and knows how the plants have been raised.
Where plants are bought-in from a garden centre, however, there is no
way of knowing how they were raised or what treatment they received
during propagation. There is no physical difference in appearance
between good plants and those at risk. The bolting is irreversible and
may vary in severity from one or two plants to the total crop being lost.
Crops that are most affected include celery, celeriac, cauliflower, broccoli, brussels sprouts, beetroot, spinach, fennel, shallots and onions.

STORING

- Most vegetables and fruits are best eaten fresh. However, the option of freezing is wonderful – I usually freeze peas, beans, tomatoes and anything that has a short life, usually blanching them first or rendering them into sauce, as for tomatoes. There is no need for me to give instructions for freezing each vegetable. However, some vegetables would occupy too much freezer space and there are other, traditional ways of storing them (eg drying and tying up onions); where there is a particular way of storing, I give instructions. Some vegetables are left in the ground until needed, and I mention this where relevant. Many can also be pickled, of course, but this is not my area of expertise, so I leave that to the cooks.

HOW TO GROW

CROP BY CROP

PERENNIAL CROPS

Perennials are crops that come back each year from the first planting. They are not part of the annual rotation scheme. They can often last, and continue to produce, for many years.

ASPARAGUS

*DIFFICULT

Asparagus is a very fine vegetable and needs the best of soil, the best of weather, and the best management. Can be grown from seed or juvenile plants, but requires a lot of patience.

HOW TO GROW

It is best to grow from plants rather than seed. You could source plants (crowns) from any good garden centre, but it's better to order them in advance as they are not readily available. I find it best to source from specialist growers who advertise in gardening magazines.

Plants

Best time to plant: spring months, March/April.

Latest time to plant: early May.

Best aspect: south, sheltered, sunny.

Best soil: deep, well-drained, well-cultivated, rich, stone-free soil.

Soil preparation: it is essential to remove any large stones and any perennial weeds; well-rotted manure or compost should also be added and mixed well with the soil.

Space between plants: 45cm (18in).

Distance betweeen rows: 120cm (4ft).

Depth of planting: 15–20cm (6–8in).

How to plant: dig out a trench about 25–30cm (10–12in) deep, and put plants on top of loosened soil – they need to be well below ground in order to blanch. Cover over, to leave a flat, even surface. When they appear above ground level, earth-up again to form a drill.

Growing situations: grown in a trench in the garden.

Best varieties: Connover's Colossal, Martha Washington, Mammoth.

Number of plants required to give a good yield: 10–12.

MANAGEMENT

- Stake up the ferns when they are about 60cm (2ft) high.
- Remove weeds. Any soil removed in hoeing (or harvesting) should be replaced the following spring to keep the height of the drill.
- In September, after cropping, cut back the withering ferns – put on compost heap.

PESTS AND DISEASES

Pests: *Slugs* can be a problem as can *asparagus beetle*, but good crops can be grown in spite of these if management instructions are followed.

Diseases: *Asparagus rust* – no way of getting rid of it, but cut out any diseased ferns; they will look rusty in colour.

HARVESTING

Average yield: 2 harvestable spears per year per plant on average (there will be many other spears, but these are allowed to develop into ferns, which are adult foliage that provide the plant with food reserves for the following year).

Life span of plant: 10–12 years.

When to harvest: varies, but usually April–May.

How to harvest: cut with a knife – holding the tip in one hand, stick the knife into the ground at an angle and try to cut at the base (it's a bit hit and miss); don't over-harvest – leave at least 2 spears on the plant to encourage future growth (if over-cut, there will be nothing left for the following year).

Good points: A long-lasting plant. Very popular vegetable.

Bad points: Can be fussy regarding soil and site. Needs a stone-free soil. Slow to produce first crop.

DO

- Get a good variety from a reliable source.
- Plant in a warm, sheltered place.
- Provide good drainage.
- Clear off all perennial weeds.
- Add in plenty manure or compost.
- Stake the foliage.

DON'T

- Plant in a poor, badly drained soil.
- Get plants of doubtful quality.
- Plant into stony soil.
- Plant too shallow.
- Allow weeds to develop.
- Harvest spears in first year.

GLOBE ARTICHOKES

*EASY

There are two types of artichoke grown in Ireland, the large thistle-like globe artichoke and the lesser known Jerusalem artichoke (see Annuals), grown like potatoes. They are from completely different families, but have a few common requirements – good soil and plenty of sun. The globe artichoke is a reliable cropper, is ornamental and grows to a height of up to 1.8 metres (6ft). It dies down every autumn and the remains of the plant can be put into the compost heap.

HOW TO GROW

Growing from seed is an option, but not easy. Most gardeners grow from young plants (offsets – small plants that grow at the base of the parent plant). They can be sourced at good garden centres in spring.

Plants

Best time to plant: end of March/early April.

Latest time to plant: end April.

Best aspect: south or south-west; shelter is essential, as plants can easily be blown over.

Best soil: deep, fertile, well-drained loam.

Soil preparation: dig deeply and incorporate dung or compost.

Space between plants: at least 120cm (4ft) between plants and 90cm (3ft) from other crops.

Depth of planting: crown or bud should be at ground level.

Growing situations: on the flat, drills, raised beds (but they grow very tall); can also be grown in an ornamental garden.

Best varieties: Green Globe, Purple Globe.

Number of plants required to give a good yield: put in several, say up to 4, if you have the space.

MANAGEMENT

- Stake in windy areas.
- Cut back the old, dead shoots in autumn and put on compost heap.
- Keep weed-free.
- Add compost or dung in early spring.
- **Disbudding**: if too many buds develop and size is small, then remove up to one third of them while they are still small to encourage greater growth – this applies if you like larger buds to eat.
- Water in dry weather – important when buds are swelling.
- **Watch out for early flowering**: the globes must never be allowed to open and come into flower as this exhausts the plant and reduces the chance of the remaining globes swelling to full size. Pick them if they are about to open.

PESTS AND DISEASES

Pests: *Slugs* attack at the emerging stages in spring and also the developing buds during summer. Hand-pick them off. *Aphids* may attack, but do not cause serious damage; spray with washing-up/water mixture.

Diseases: no serious diseases.

HARVESTING
Time from planting to first harvest: about 15 months.
Expected yields: 10–12 globes per plant over the season.
Time of harvesting: July–September.

- Harvest when globes are big enough but before the flower opens – the tips are a blue or purple colour.

Good points: Reasonably hardy. Lasts for 5–6 years. Reliable croppers.
Bad points: Slow to become established. Shades out other crops.

RHUBARB

*EASY

Is it a fruit or a vegetable? Whatever you choose to call it (it's actually a modified petiole, ie a stem of a leaf), it's a very popular garden crop that will tolerate neglect and continue to give a crop year after year.

HOW TO GROW
Usually grown from stools, which are taken from an existing plant. It should have at least one bud/eye. Make sure they come from a good cropping source – if you get them from a friend you need to check with them. Can also be propagated from seeds, but this is a much longer process.

Plants

Best time to plant: November/December.

Latest time to plant: January for early varieties (if the weather is good); March for main crop.

Best aspect: southerly or south-westerly.

Best soil: deep, rich, well-prepared, medium to heavy loam.

Soil preparation: dig deeply; add in manure or compost and mix well. Remove roots of perennial weeds.

Space between stools/plants: 60–90cm (2–3ft).

Depth of planting: make sure the bud is at soil level.

Growing situations: on the flat, raised beds, big containers.

Best varieties: *early crop* – Timperley Early; *main crop* – Victoria, Hawke's Champagne, Glaskin's Perpetual.

Number of plants required to give good yield: 6–8.

MANAGEMENT

- Keep weeds under control, especially perennials.
- Water during dry spell.
- Give a dressing of well-rotted manure or compost every January/February.
- In the first year, pick one or two stalks only.
- **Bolting**: a strong, flowering shoot will sometimes emerge from the centre of some plants shortly after the first stalks grow, usually after a mild winter. Cut off the flowering stem as soon as noticed, otherwise the plant expends its energy in seed production.

PESTS AND DISEASES

Remarkably free of these.

HARVESTING

Time from planting to harvesting: 12 months.

When to harvest: *early crop* mid-March; *main crop* May-June; *latest crop* September.

Latest time for picking: September (if you over-pick, you weaken the plant for coming years).

• **Life span**: well-managed plants will last indefinitely, while neglected ones will give poor returns and die off after a number of years.

PROPAGATION

To propagate: divide the roots with a spade or sharp knife, ensuring there is a live bud and good root in each part. Do this only if you want to plant more, or give to a friend, or if the space is getting over-crowded; otherwise leave it alone.

From seeds: I don't really advise doing this unless you have your heart set on it. It will take 3–4 years before a reasonable crop is produced. Sow in a seed tray in March; will propagate at about 10°C (50–55°F). Cover with 1–2cm (½in) soil; should germinate in 3 weeks or so, grow on inside and harden-off; plant outside in May–June, 30cm x 30cm apart. Select out the best plants when planting out – look for good colour and vigour.

Good points: Crops year after year. Tolerant of pests and diseases. Survives despite lack of care.

Bad points: Can become a haven for perennial weeds. Needs a large area of ground. Tends to run to seed some years. Leaves are poisonous, but can be put on compost heap.

DO

- Plant in a well-prepared, rich soil.
- Add dung or compost.
- Provide good drainage.
- Get roots from a reliable source.
- Plant an early and late variety.
- Give plenty space to develop.
- Dig up and divide every 6–8 years.

DON'T

- Plant in poor soil.
- Plant in poorly drained soil.
- Plant too deep or too shallow.
- Plant too close together.
- Over-pick the first year.

TOP TIP

Plant two varieties – early crop, main crop. Pick the early one first and allow the main crop to develop. Then pick the main crop and allow the early one to build up reserves for the following spring.

ANNUAL CROPS

BEANS
BROAD BEANS

*VERY EASY

These are beans where the seeds are taken out of the pod to eat; the bean sits in what looks like cotton wool. They deserve to be more popular in Ireland as they are very hardy, one of the first vegetable seeds to be sown each year and do not need staking. Also very high in food value, especially protein. They are best eaten young.

HOW TO GROW

Seeds

Earliest time to sow: *indoors* first half of February; harden-off before transplanting outdoors. *Outdoors* mid-April (no transplanting needed).

Latest time to sow: end of June.

Best time to sow: mid-April.

Depth of sowing: 5cm (2in).

Germination time: 12–14 days.

Lifespan of seed: 2–3 years.

Successional sowings: make 2–3 sowings in the year, at 1-month intervals.

Plants

Best time to plant: early April (*indoors* February).

Stage of growth: when they are about 12–15cm (4–6in) tall.

Best aspect: south-facing, well-sheltered.

Best soil: deep, rich, light to medium loam.

Soil preparation: dig deep, and add manure or compost.

Spacing between plants: 20cm (8in).

Distance between rows: 90cm (3ft).

Depth of planting: to soil mark on the stem.

Growing situations: in drills, on the flat, raised beds.

Best varieties: Aquadulce, Early Longpod, White Windsor.

Number of plants needed for good yield: 10–12 per sowing.

MANAGEMENT

- Make successional sowings every month.
- In very exposed situations, stake.
- Control weeds.
- Control pests, such as slugs.
- Pinch out the tops of stalks to prevent disease developing.

PESTS AND DISEASES

Pests: *Black bean aphid* infests the growing tip of the plant. This pest can be controlled by pinching out the growing point of the bean plant as soon as they are noticed. The *bean weevil*, which eats the edges of the bean plant, does very little damage and can be ignored. *Slugs* – put out traps. *Rabbits* and *pigeons* will attack if nothing else is available; it's worth netting to prevent.

Diseases: A disease called *chocolate spot* occurs some years, especially wet years, and its name is descriptive. Pinch out the top 4–5cm (2in) off the top of the plant as the chocolate spot appears; this also helps to control aphids.

HARVESTING

Average yield per plant: 15–20 pods.

Time from sowing to harvesting: 4 months.

When to harvest: pull off a pod and taste – if the bean inside is soft and sweet, it's ready to harvest. If sweetness is gone, it's over-ripe – if left unharvested, they lose their sweetness and become tough.

How to harvest: discard pod (to compost) and eat the bean.

Good points: Very hardy. Not fussy about soils. Will tolerate cold spells.

Bad points: Susceptible to growing-point pests and diseases. They over-mature very fast.

DO

- Sow early into well-prepared ground.
- Space seed 20–25cm (8–10in) apart in single row.
- Sow seed 5cm (2in) deep.
- Make later sowings at 3- to 4-week intervals.

DON'T

- Sow in ground where peas or beans were grown in previous 3 years.
- Sow in cold areas with poor soil.
- Allow weeds to grow.
- Allow pigeons and rabbits to get at plants.

*** TOP TIP

Pick pods, whether they are needed or not, as this promotes further fresh growth.

DWARF FRENCH BEANS

*MEDIUM

A member of the Leguminosae or pea (pulse) family. A popular but not very hardy crop to grow. Likes warm air and rich, warm soil conditions. Can be transplanted or sown direct, and 2–3 sowings in the year are needed. There is no need to stake.

HOW TO GROW

They are best started off as seeds indoors but can also be sown outdoors. As they are sensitive to frost, you need to watch weather conditions carefully.

Seeds

Earliest time to sow: *inside* end March; *outdoors* April (no transplanting needed for these, thin-out instead).

Latest time to sow: end of June.

Best time to sow: mid-April.

Depth of sowing: 5cm (2in).

Germination time: 12 days.

Lifespan of seeds: 2 years.

Successional sowings: make sowings at 4-week intervals until end of June.

Plants

Best time to plant: early April for those sown indoors after hardening-off.

Latest time to plant: end May.

Stage of growth: first rough-leaf stage, after hardening-off.

Best aspect: southerly, but sheltered.

Best soil: deep, rich, medium loam.

Soil preparation: dig deep and incorporate manure and compost.

Space between plants: 10cm (4in).

Distance between rows: 60cm (24in).

Depth of planting: to soil mark on stem.

Growing situations: raised beds, drills, on the flat.

Best varieties: Masterpiece, The Prince. These are both green, but there are coloured varieties available. They all taste equally good, but people find the colour variation attractive.

Number of plants needed for a good yield: 20–25.

MANAGEMENT

- Water in dry weather.
- Make a second sowing 4–5 weeks after first.
- Harden off indoor-raised plants before planting out.
- Keep weeds under control by hand and by hoe.
- Give liquid feed as plants start cropping.

PESTS AND DISEASES

Pests: *Slugs* attack at the seedling stage; slug trap should be put out as beans are emerging. *Rabbits* graze the young plants, *crows* pull up the germinating plants, and *pigeons* will graze the leaves and young pods. Nets will give protection from rabbits and birds.

Diseases: *Botrytis* is the most common disease and is most common in cold, damp weather. Ensure good ventilation and do not sow seed too close together.

HARVESTING

Average yield per plant: 10–12 pods, but greatly varied depending on variety.

Time from sowing to harvesting: 14 weeks.

When to harvest: when the pods are about pencil-thick.

How to harvest: pull off pods; if the pod snaps on bending, the beans are still edible, but if the pod bends without breaking they have probably gone tough and are not good for cooking.

Good points: Very distinctive taste. Can be grown inside or outside. Can be transplanted.

Bad points: Susceptible to cold weather. Will go over-mature fairly fast. Not able to compete with weeds.

DO

- Sow when soil temperatures are right.
- Sow in rich, well-prepared ground.
- Sow early crops under protection.
- Plant in a well-sheltered area.
- Add manure or compost before sowing or planting.
- Keep weeds under control.
- Provide protection from rabbits and birds.
- Sow seed 5cm (2in) deep.
- Seed spaced 10–12cm (4–5in) apart.
- Allow 30cm (1ft) between adjacent rows.

DON'T

- Sow in ground where peas or beans grew in the previous three years.
- Sow until frost danger is gone and soil is warm enough.
- Sow too deeply or too shallowly.
- Sow adjacent rows too near each other.
- Allow rabbits and birds access to plants.
- Allow weeds get out of control.

***TOP TIP

Sow indoors in pots or seed trays and transplant out when warm enough.

SCARLET RUNNER BEANS
*MODERATELY EASY

A little-known crop in Ireland, of the Leguminosae (pea) family, which deserves to be more popular. A climber that needs stakes or support, is ornamental and often used as a boundary between vegetable and flower garden. Well worth growing for its good yield, reliability and great uses in cooking.

HOW TO GROW

These seeds are quite large and need specific spaces between seeds and rows.

Seeds

Earliest time to sow: *indoors* early April, for transplanting, usually outdoors; *outdoors* early May.

Latest time to sow: *indoors* mid-May; *outdoors* late June.

Best time to sow: mid-April.

Depth of sowing: 5cm (2in).

Distance between seeds: 22–25cm (9–10in).

Distance between rows: 1.8 metres (6ft).

Germination time: 10–14 days.

Lifespan of seeds: 2–3 years.

Successional sowings: 2–3 sowings per year, about a month apart; about 18–20 seeds or plants per sowing.

Plants

Best time to plant: early May (when risk of frost is gone).

Latest time to plant: end June.

Stage of growth: first rough-leaf stage.

Best aspect: southerly. *Shelter*: anything that protects against wind is important; this also helps pollination.

Best soil: rich, deep, well-drained loam.

Soil preparation: dig deep and remove any perennial weeds before adding in manure and compost.

Space between plants: 22–25cm (9–10in).

Distance between rows: 1.8 metres (6ft).

Depth of planting: to soil mark on stem.

Growing situations: drills, on the flat, but too high for raised beds; can be grown in polytunnel, but they can grow too high and cause too much shading.

Best varieties: Scarlet Emperor, Crusader. A number of non-climbing varieties are available, but are not as prolific as the climbing type.

Number of plants needed for a good yield: 15–20 per sowing.

MANAGEMENT

• Support either with canes, wire netting, or chicken wire. Place them at the time of planting.
• Harden-off plants before planting-out if raised inside.
• Pick pods as they mature.
• Water in dry weather.

PESTS AND DISEASES

Pests: Apart from *slugs* and *birds*, remarkably free of pests and diseases. Birds pick up the seeds and young plants, so use nets at the outset and make sure you plant deeply enough, 5cm (2in). Slugs are controlled by putting out slug traps.

HARVESTING

Average yield per plant: 1 kilo (2.2lbs) beans per plant.
Time from sowing to harvest: 12–14 weeks.
When to harvest: July from early sowing; August/September from main sowing. Harvest while pods are still fleshy and crisp, but before the seed forms within the pod. *Signs of over-maturity*: the seeds will be apparent in the pod if it is opened and the pod itself will not snap if bent.

Good points: Ornamental as well as edible. Bulks up well when grown well. Not subject to many pests or diseases.
Bad points: Needs staking or support. Frost-tender. Difficult to get established. Tall varieties not suitable for raised beds.

DO

- Sow in a warm, sheltered situation.
- Sow in a rich, well-prepared soil.
- Sow when risk of frost has gone.
- Sow seed 5cm (2in) deep.
- Sow seed 22–25cm (9–10in) apart.
- Protect from pests.
- Provide support when plants are 15cm (6in) high.

DON'T

- Sow or plant in a cold, poor soil.
- Sow too early while frosts are likely.
- Sow too deep or too shallow.
- Sow or plant too close together.
- Put rows too close to each other.

***TOP TIP

Pick off pods when large enough, whether they are needed or not, as pods swelling with seed will exhaust the plant and stop flowering and pod production.

BEETROOT

*EASY

A popular vegetable that in Ireland is used more often as a salad than as a hot, cooked vegetable, though perhaps habits are changing in this respect as people are finding that it is wonderful baked in the oven in foil. Rather easy to grow, as long as it is not sown too early, when it tends to bolt.

HOW TO GROW

Sow seeds outdoors in the ground where the plant is to grow. Not suitable for transplanting. Seeds may produce 1–3 plants; in this case, thin-out.

Seeds

Earliest time to sow: mid-April onwards.

Latest time to sow: middle to end of July.

Best time to sow: late April.

Best aspect: warm, southerly aspect, sheltered.

Best soil: deep, rich, medium loam, well prepared.

Soil preparation: dig deep, remove perennial weeds and prepare a fine seedbed. Dig in manure and/or compost; both are beneficial.

Depth of sowing: 1cm (¾in).

Space between seeds: sow thinly, 1cm (1/2in) apart.

Distance between rows: 30–35cm (12–14in).

Germination time: 2–3 weeks.

Lifespan of seed: 3 years.

Thinning-out: thin-out, leaving the strong ones to grow, at roughly 10–15cm (4–6in) apart. Put others on compost heap.

Growing situations: drills, on the flat, raised beds.

Successional sowings: sow the first crop in April and the main crop in early June.

Best varieties: Boltardy (best early variety); Detroit, Avonearly, Cylindra, Cheltenham Greentop are better for main crops.

Number of plants needed for a good yield: 30–40.

MANAGEMENT
- Thin-out plants to 10–12cm (4–6in) apart, at second-leaf stage.
- Keep weeds under control.
- Put out slug traps.

PESTS AND DISEASES
Pests: *Slugs* will attack at all stages of growth, so put out slug traps in damp weather. Where *rabbits* are present, put up nets at sowing time as they will graze on beetroot plants.

Diseases: largely free of diseases.

HARVESTING
Time from sowing to harvest: 3 months for earlies and 4 months for main crop.

When to harvest: you can harvest some when immature, about 2cm (1in) diameter, especially for salads. They are mature and ready for harvesting when they are about 3cm (1½in) in diameter – though they can grow to 12cm and still be tender – and should be harvested before they become tough; test this by pulling the largest one out of the ground and cutting it across the centre – if there are white rings through the flesh, then it has gone past its best (you can eat them, but they take longer to cook); pull up the smaller ones immediately and use; main crops, sown later, are usually stored for later use.

How to harvest: pull them up, twist (don't cut) the leaves off.

Storing: don't leave in the ground in winter; store in either sand or peat in a container that is frost-proof and rat-proof.

Good points: Will grow in a wide range of soils. Very few diseases attack beetroot. Best when used fresh; if stored they lose some moisture and get a little tough.

Bad points: Tends to bolt if sown too early. Subject to Boron deficiency. Not completely winter hardy.

DO

- Sow in rich soil.
- Sow after frost danger is gone.
- Prepare the soil well before sowing seed.
- Choose a good variety.
- Sow thinly.
- Thin-out in time.
- Protect from pests.

DON'T

- Sow too early.
- Sow in poor soil.
- Sow in cold, frosty situations.
- Sow too thickly.
- Allow weeds to grow.

***TOP TIP

Best early variety is Boltardy, which can be sown early (first week of April) and will not bolt.

BROCCOLI

A member of the brassica (cabbage) family and a close relation of cauliflower. There are two types: a spring/summer type and a winter/spring type.

(spring/summer)

*MEDIUM– DIFFICULT

HOW TO GROW

Can be sown indoors in a seed tray or outside in a seedbed. Prick-out to individual cells and harden-off before planting-out.

Seeds

Earliest time to sow: mid-February, in heat.

Latest time to sow: mid- to end June.

Best time to sow: mid-April.

Depth of sowing: 1cm (½in). Sow thinly to about 1cm (½in) apart.

Germination time: 10 days.

Lifespan of seed: about 5 years provided it is stored in an airtight jar and kept in a cool place.

Successional sowings: every 4–5 weeks to end of June.

Plants

Best time to plant: from early April.

Latest time to plant: end July.

Stage of growth: 2–3 rough-leaf stage.

Best aspect: south and well-sheltered.

Best soil: well-drained, rich, light to medium loam.

Soil preparation: dig deep, incorporating manure and compost.

Spacing between plants: 30cm (12in).

Distance between rows: 45cm (18in).

Depth of planting: to soil mark on stem.

Growing situations: can be grown in raised beds, drills or on the flat.

Best varieties: Romanesco, Corvette, Comet (all F1 hybrids).

MANAGEMENT

- Transplant at 3–4 rough-leaf stage.
- Harden-off indoor-raised plants.
- When harvested, pull up stumps and put on compost heap.

PESTS AND DISEASES

Pests: *Pigeons and rabbits*: control by nets. *Slugs*: put out slug traps. *Aphids*: spray with washing-up liquid/water solution as soon as they appear. *Caterpillars*: remove by hand or spray off with a salt and water solution.

HARVESTING

Time from sowing to harvest: approximately 12 weeks.

When to harvest: when the head has formed.

Good point: Grows and matures fast.

Bad points: Runs to seed very quickly if not harvested on time. Will not grow in poor ground.

DO

- Plant into rich, well-drained ground.

- Give plenty of space between plants.
- Give plenty of water in dry weather.
- Earth-up plants a few weeks after transplanting.

DON'T

- Plant into poor, cold soil.
- Plant out too early.
- Plant too close together.
- Allow weeds get out of control.

***TOP TIP

To get continuity of supply, make 2–3 sowings and 2 trans-plantings (from each sowing, pick out the best plants first and plant out, then two weeks later plant out the remainder). The date of transplanting has a bigger influence on the date of harvest than the date of sowing.

(winter-sprouting)

*EASY

A close relation to the spring/summer broccoli, but very hardy; survives winter well to produce edible spears or sprouts in March/April.

HOW TO GROW

Seeds

Sow thinly outdoors in a seedbed and transplant.

Best time to sow: between end of April and early May.

Depth of sowing: 1cm (½in). Sow thinly to about 1cm (½in) apart.

Germination time: 10 days.

Lifespan of seeds: about 5 years provided they are stored in an airtight jar and kept in a cool place.

Successional sowings: usually only one.

Plants

Earliest time to plant: end June to mid-July.

Latest time to plant: end July.

Best time to plant: early June.

Stage of growth: 2–3 rough-leaf stage.

Best aspect: southerly or south-westerly.

Best soil: light to medium, well-drained, rich loam.

Soil preparation: dig in manure or compost before planting.

Space between plants: 45cm (18in).

Distance between rows: 60cm (2ft).

Depth of planting: to soil mark on stem.

Growing situations: in the ground outdoors; gets too big in glasshouse or polytunnel.

Best varieties: Purple Sprouting, White Sprouting (open-pollinated).

Number of plants needed for a good yield: 20.

MANAGEMENT

Earth-up once, especially in exposed situations.

PESTS AND DISEASES

Pests: *Slugs* can be problem, so use slug traps. *Caterpillars* should be controlled by hand before they grow large; or spray on a salt-and-water solution. *Birds* and *butterflies* will attack: put up netting.

Diseases: fairly free of diseases.

HARVESTING

Time from sowing to harvest: 8–9 months.

When to harvest: March/April or when spears are about finger-sized, before the flower opens.

How to harvest: pluck off spears that are on the point of flowering. Keep picking and don't allow the plant to flower.

BRUSSELS SPROUTS
*CHALLENGING

A winter-hardy, tall-growing brassica that is hard to grow well. It needs wide spacing and takes a long time from sowing till harvest. Seeds may be sown directly into the ground or raised in a seedbed and transplanted. Needs plenty of space, deep, well-prepared ground and protection from pigeons. Best trying initially with bought-in plants.

HOW TO GROW

Seeds

Outdoors, plant in a seedbed or in the spot where you want the sprouts to grow. Indoors, sow in a seed tray.

Earliest time to sow: *indoors* early March; *outdoors* mid-April.

Latest time to sow: *indoors and outdoors* mid-April, where they are to mature; where 2–3 seeds are sown, thin-out to a single plant at second rough-leaf stage. If you intend transplanting, sow a week earlier (early April) as disturbing them delays maturity.

Best time to sow: early April.

Depth of sowing: 1cm (½in).

Germination time: 10–12 days.

Lifespan of seed: 5 years.

Successional sowings: one sowing; if sowing different varieties sow both at same time.

Plants

Earliest time to plant: early May.

Latest time to plant: end of June.

Best time to plant: early June.

Stage of growth: at 3–4 rough-leaf stage.

Best aspect: southerly and sheltered.

Best soil: deep, well-drained, rich medium loam. Sprouts are heavy feeders.

Soil preparation: dig deep and incorporate manure and compost. For seedbed, break up all lumps and rake off to a smooth finish.

Space between plants: 60cm (2ft).

Distance between rows: 60–90cm (2–3ft).

Depth of planting: to soil mark on stem.

Growing situations: raised bed, on the flat or in drills.

Best varieties: Rampart, Fortress, Peer Gynt.

Number of plants needed for a good yield: about 15.

MANAGEMENT

- Earth-up soil around lower part of stems when plants are 30cm (1ft) high.

- Control weeds, pests and diseases.
- Water in dry weather.

PESTS AND DISEASES

Pests: *Slugs* can be a problem from the seedling stage right up to harvest time. Put out slug traps before the slugs get into the plant. *Aphids* in sprouts can be very serious and should be sprayed with a solution of water and washing-up liquid as soon as the first aphid is noticed. *Rabbits* and *pigeons* should be controlled by putting up nets.

Diseases: There are numerous diseases that affect brussels sprouts, but with proper rotation these are seldom a problem. The more serious diseases are *club root*, *internal browning*, *white blister* and *ring spot*, but are too rare to concern us here.

HARVESTING

Time from sowing to harvest: 7–9 months.

How to harvest: leave on plant until required; pick as they mature. The lower sprouts mature first, so pick from the bottom of the plant.

Good points: Winter hardy. Resistant to most pests and diseases.

Bad points: Long growing season. Slow to mature.

DO

- Sow and plant in ground where no brassicas were grown in previous three years.
- Sow in deep, rich ground.
- Sow on time.

- Sow seed 1–2cm (½in) deep.
- Plant plants well spaced at least 60cm x 60cm (2ft x 2ft).
- Give protection from pests.

DON'T

- Sow too early or too late.
- Plant into poor, badly prepared ground.
- Allow weeds to get out of control.

When sprouts are finished cropping, leave the plants there and in spring they will produce fresh green shoots that can be cooked as spring greens.

CABBAGE

Traditionally, probably the most popular vegetable in Ireland and there are varieties for every season. Has had a very bad press in recent years, probably because of the old-style cooking method – boiling. Nowadays, people prefer to shred it and eat it raw or very lightly cooked, eg as a stir-fry. It is easy to grow and provides an almost year-round vegetable, which is very valuable. I think it will become popular again in forthcoming years. Cabbage is popular with rabbits and pigeons, and pests such as caterpillars and aphids will seek out a crop in any garden. For specific growing instructions see under separate headings – spring cabbage, winter cabbage etc. 'Brassica' is the family name of cabbages, and includes savoy, kale, broccoli, cauliflower, brussels sprouts, turnips and swedes. Being of the same family, they are all subject to the same diseases, whether on the leaves, roots, stems or seeds. There should be a gap of at least three years – longer is better – between any two crops of these being planted in any site to prevent spread of disease and reduce risk of pest damage. This also helps to balance the uptake of nutrients from the soil.

HOW TO GROW

See specific details below on seasonal and other cabbages. Though they are seasonal, the growing times overlap, of course. You will need to deal with several types of seasonal cabbages at any given time, for example, summer cabbage may still be cropping in September when autumn cabbage is beginning to crop or is in mid-crop. It is important to grow the varieties in the season for which they are intended, otherwise they may fail to form a head, bolt, or be wiped out by frost or cold weather.

PESTS AND DISEASES

Pests: *Slugs* are a threat to the cabbage plant at all stages of growth; use slug traps. *Aphids* can cause serious damage in warm weather and are controlled by using a water and washing-up liquid spray when first noticed. *Caterpillars* usually occur in late summer/autumn, but can occur any time; either hand-pick off the eggs (on underside of leaf) or small caterpillars as soon as noticed or spray with salt and water.

Diseases: The most serious disease is *club root* (or *finger and toe*), which affects the roots. There is no cure, but rotation of crops is a good preventative.

(spring cabbage)

*EASY

Spring cabbage is sown in late July and planted out in the autumn – it remains in the ground over winter to start growing again in the spring. The plants must be strong enough to withstand the winter and yet not too big that bolting might occur. The correct variety is vital. Though easy to grow, it is hard to keep it free of weeds.

HOW TO GROW

Sow thinly in seedbed and transplant.

Seeds

Earliest time to sow: late July.

Latest time to sow: early August.

Best time to sow: last week July.

Sowing depth: 1cm (½in).

Germination time: 8–10 days.

Lifespan of seed: 3–5 years.

Successional sowings: one sowing.

Plants

Best time to plant: end of September/early October.

Latest time to plant: mid-October.

Stage of growth: 2–3 rough-leaf stage, or slightly more.

Best aspect: southerly and well-sheltered.

Best soil: well-drained, deep rich loam.

Soil preparation: dig 20cm (8–9in) deep, adding in compost and dung.

Space between plants: 25–30cm (10–12in).

Distance between rows: 45cm (18in).

Depth of planting: to soil mark on stem.

Growing situations: drills, on the flat, raised beds (though they look untidy over winter).

Best varieties: Flower of Spring, Ellam's Early, Durham Early, Early Offenham.

MANAGEMENT

- Protect from rabbits and birds with nets.
- Monitor for slugs and put out traps.
- Earth-up 4–6 weeks after transplanting.
- Keep free of weeds.

PESTS AND DISEASES

See under Cabbages p72.

HARVESTING

Time from sowing to harvest: 7–8 months. Initially the heads are quite small, then they will be bigger as the season progresses.

Good points: First crop available in spring. Very hardy.

Bad points: A long time in ground (6 months). Leaves ground weedy.

DO

- Sow correct variety.
- Sow on correct date.
- Transplant at correct time.

- Protect from pests.
- Earth-up after planting.

DON'T

- Plant where brassicas were grown in previous three years.
- Allow weeds to grow.
- Plant in poorly drained land.

(summer cabbage)

*EASY

A fast-maturing crop, producing a small, firm head, but quick to bolt. Though plants of summer cabbages are available at garden centres, there can be problems sometimes with them as they may not have been properly hardened-off and may bolt or die after planting out.

HOW TO GROW

Seeds

Earliest time to sow: *indoors* mid-February; *outdoors* early March.

Latest time to sow: mid-May.

Best time to sow: mid-March.

Depth of sowing: 1cm (½in).

Germination time: 8–10 days.

Lifespan of seeds: 5 years.

Successional sowings: every 4–5 weeks.

Plants

Earliest time to plant: early April.

Latest time to plant: end of June.

Best time to plant: end of April.

Stage of growth: 2–3 rough-leaf stage.

Best aspect: southerly or south westerly, with shelter.

Best soil: well-drained, light to medium rich loam.

Soil preparation: dig out perennial weeds, add dung or compost.

Space between plants: 28–30cm (10–12in).

Distance between rows: 45cm (18in).

Depth of planting: to soil mark on stem.

Growing situations: on the flat, drills, raised beds; outdoors.

Best varieties: Greyhound, Hispi, Golden Acre, Primo.

MANAGEMENT

* Harden-off indoor-raised plants.
* Protect from birds and rabbits with nets.
* Water in dry weather.
* Control weeds.
* Control slugs with slug trap at all stages.
* Monitor for aphids and spray with a water and washing-up liquid dilution.

PESTS AND DISEASES

See under Cabbages p72.

HARVESTING

Time from sowing to harvest: 12–14 weeks.

When to harvest: harvest when the head feels hard and the outer leaves are beginning to split; you can also harvest before that stage when heads are quite small.

Good points: Fast-maturing crop. Not as susceptible to pests and diseases as later crops. Small, compact heads.

Bad points: Runs to seed fast after reaching maturity. Hard to get plants at right stage for transplanting.

DO

• Sow the proper variety.

• Sow seed in late February to mid-March.

• Harden-off plants.

• Plant close together 25cm (10in) apart in rows 35–40cm (14–16in) apart.

• Sow and plant in well-drained, well-prepared land.

• Use animal manures or compost where possible.

• Protect early crops from frost.

DON'T

• Sow seed late.

• Sow too early.

• Sow in poor soil.

• Plant too deeply.

(autumn cabbage)

*MEDIUM TO DIFFICULT

These heads are bigger than summer cabbages and do not bolt or run to seed as fast. They can last up to the time of the first autumn frosts, usually November.

HOW TO GROW

Seeds

Sow outdoors in a seedbed, seed tray or cellular trays. One sowing per season.

Earliest time to sow: early April.

Latest time to sow: mid-May.

Best time to sow: end of April.

Depth of sowing: 1cm (½in).

Germination time: 8–10 days.

Lifespan of seeds: 5 years.

Successional sowings: one sowing.

Plants

Earliest time to plant: early June.

Latest time to plant: end of June.

Best time to plant: mid-June.

Stage of growth: 2–3 rough-leaf stage.

Best aspect: southerly, but well sheltered.

Best soil: free draining, deep, fertile medium loam

Soil preparation: dig deep and remove perennial weeds before incorporating manure and compost.

Space between plants: 30–35cm (12–14in).

Distance between rows: 45cm (18in).

Depth of planting: to soil mark on stem.

Growing situations: on the flat, drills, raised beds.

Best varieties: Winnigistadt, Cape Horn, Stonehead. These do particularly well in Irish conditions.

MANAGEMENT

- Earth-up 4–6 weeks after planting.

- Transplant at 3–4 rough-leaf stage.
- Protect from birds and rabbits, using nets.
- Monitor for slugs and use slug traps.
- Water in dry weather.

PESTS AND DISEASES

See Cabbages p72.

HARVESTING

Time from sowing to harvest: approx 16 weeks.

When to harvest: September–October.

Good points: Bigger heads than summer types. Tend to last longer before running to seed.

Bad point: Very susceptible to caterpillars (more so than summer cabbage).

DO

- Sow the correct varieties.
- Sow at the time specified.
- Sow seed 1cm (½in) deep.
- Transplant at the correct time.
- Space the plants 30–35cm (12–14in) apart.
- Allow 45cm (18in) between rows.
- Earth-up rows about one month after planting.
- Protect from pests and diseases.

DON'T

- Plant too close together.
- Plant too late.
- Sow or plant the wrong variety.

(winter cabbage)

*MEDIUM TO DIFFICULT

All winter cabbages are hardy, but they must be sown in time so as to become established and grow before the temperatures drop too low. Winter cabbages are put in the ground very early – even earlier than autumn cabbages – as their growing season is very long.

HOW TO GROW

Seeds

Sow outdoors in a seedbed, seed tray or cellular tray. One sowing per season.

Best time to sow: end of March to mid-May.

Latest time to sow: mid-May.

Depth of sowing: 1cm (½in).

Germination time: 8–10 days.

Lifespan of seeds: 5 years.

Successional sowings: one sowing per variety.

Plants

Best time to plant: mid-June to mid-July.

Latest time to plant: early July.

Stage of growth: 2–3 rough-leaf stage.

Best aspect: southerly and well sheltered.

Best soil: deep, well-drained, rich medium loam.

Soil preparation: dig deep, incorporating manure or compost.

Space between plants: 30–35cm (12–14in).

Distance between rows: 45cm (18in).

Depth of planting: to soil mark on stem.

Growing situations: on the flat, drills, raised beds.

Best varieties: Stonehead, Celsa, Celtic, January King.

MANAGEMENT

- Transplant at 3–4 rough-leaf stage.
- Protect from pests, like pigeons and rabbits, by using nets.
- Earth-up 4–6 weeks after planting.

PESTS AND DISEASES

See Cabbages p72.

HARVESTING

Time from sowing to harvest: 8 months.

When to harvest: November–February, maybe even March. Leave in ground, but will bolt in a mild spring (but your spring cabbages will be growing then!).

Good point: A winter-hardy vegetable.

Bad point: Needs plenty of space to grow.

DO

- Sow the correct variety.
- Sow seed on time, 1cm (½in) deep.
- Transplant on time into well-manured soil.
- Earth-up the drills one month after planting.
- Give protection from pests.

DON'T

- Sow too late.

- Sow the wrong variety.
- Plant too close together.
- Plant where brassicas were grown during the previous four years.

***TOP TIP

Plant where early potatoes have been dug out as the ground is already prepared and the need for manure or compost is reduced.

(red cabbage/white coleslaw)

*EASY

Red and coleslaw cabbages are grown in exactly the same way and at the same times; only the varieties differ. They are very frost-hardy.

HOW TO GROW

Seeds

Sow outdoors in a seedbed, seed tray or cellular tray. One sowing in the season is usually sufficient.

Best time to sow: end of April.

Layest time to sow: mid-May.

Depth of sowing: 1cm (½in).

Germination time: 8–10 days.

Lifespan of seeds: 5 years.

Successional sowing: one sowing.

Plants

Best time to plant: early June.

Latest time to plant: mid-July.

Stage of growth: 2–3 rough-leaf stage.

Best aspect: southerly.

Best soil: well-drained, rich, medium loam.

Soil preparation: dig deep and incorporate manure and compost.

Space between plants: 30–35cm (12–14in).

Distance between rows: 45cm (18in).

Depth of planting: to soil mark on stem.

Growing situations: can be grown in raised beds, drills or flat ground.

Best varieties: *red cabbage* Auturo; *white cabbage* Quisto, Hidena, Bartolo.

MANAGEMENT

- Use netting to protect from birds and rabbits.
- Earth-up 4–6 weeks after planting.
- Keep slugs under control.
- Watch for aphids, and destroy while numbers are small.

PESTS AND DISEASES

See Cabbages p72.

HARVESTING

Time from sowing to harvest: approx 8 months.

When to harvest: any time from November to March.

Storing: can be stored for 2–3 months in a cold situation. When taking out of store, trim off any spoilt leaves before use.

Good points: Can be grown into hard, tight head which is ideal for coleslaw. Winter hardy.

Bad points: Slow-growing. Difficult to start.

DO

- Sow correct variety.
- Give plenty space.
- Sow and transplant on time.

DON'T

- Sow or transplant too late.
- Plant too close together.

***TOP TIP

Ordinary varieties of cabbage are not suitable for making coleslaw as the green chlorophyll runs from the leaf when it is cut. The special coleslaw varieties do not suffer from this fault.

CARROTS

*MEDIUM

A great favourite with gardeners, but also very popular with the carrot-root fly! Despite this problem, good crops of carrots can be grown if the basic rules are observed. There are different types of carrot: stump-rooted, intermediate and long. I prefer to grow the intermediate because they are easier to grow than the long, and the stump-rooted tend to be greenish at the top.

HOW TO GROW

Seeds

Sow seed very thinly, 1cm (½in) apart, so as to avoid thinning if possible – thinning attracts carrot-root fly. However, you may have to thin-out to give space to allow the carrots to develop. Sowing too thinly may result in too sparse a plant stand because of poor germination or slug attack. There's some luck involved in this! Carrot seedlings do not transplant successfully. If you sow the seed indoors, let them mature indoors – sow in a seedbed in a glasshouse or polytunnel. Do not plant where carrots, parsnips, celery, celeriac, parsley have grown in the previous four years. Carrot-root fly is controlled by good rotation and hygiene practice.

Earliest time to sow: *indoors* early February; *outdoors* early March.

Latest time to sow: *outdoors* in cold areas, mid-May; in warmer areas first week of June.

Best time to sow: April.

Best aspect: southerly and sheltered.

Best soil: a rich, deep, light to medium soil.

Soil preparation: dig deep, remove all perennial weeds and clods. Do not add any dung as it causes forking. Add compost.

Depth of sowing: 1cm (½in).

Space between seeds: sow as thinly as possible.

Distance between rows: 45cm (18in).

Germination time: 14–21 days.

Lifespan of seeds: 5–6 years.

Thinning-out: at 2–4 rough-leaf stage; to 5–8cm (2–3in) apart.

Growing situations: raised beds, drills or on the flat.

Successional sowings: make at least two sowings, one early and then a main crop in April.

Best varieties: *early* Amsterdam and Nantes; *main crops* Chantanay, Autumn King and Red Elephant.

MANAGEMENT

- Prevent slug damage at seedling stage.
- Thinning-out: remove thinnings far away, 10 metres (9 yards) from remaining carrots to prevent root fly from picking up the scent. Water thoroughly before thinning-out to reduce damage to roots and reduce scent.
- Water during dry weather. Carrots can split because of uneven growth and uneven supplies of water. A dry spell, followed by a vigorous growth spurt, will cause splitting.
- Put soil up over them for protection in winter.
- Keep out rabbits – use nets.
- Control weeds with hoe and hand weeding.

PESTS AND DISEASES

Pests: The *carrot-root fly* emerges from mid-May, depending on temperatures, and lays eggs on crops of carrots, parsnips, celery and wild carrots (where they survive in nature). It is the maggot or grub that hatches out which causes the damage to carrots. The fly never rises more than 60cm (2ft) over ground level but can be carried higher by wind. You can help prevent attack by putting a wall-like barrier of close-mesh (½cm) netting around the growing site – it must be over 60cm high. Since the prevailing wind in Ireland is from the south-west and is mild, the best location to sow carrots initially is the most northerly point of your plot (thus the fly will be blow away from the crop), moving gradually south in subsequent years. Growing a few French marigolds (6–10 in a 3m site, for example) mixed in amongst the carrots offers some control, as does growing a row of onions or garlic in between the rows of carrots. These may not give 100 percent control, but there will be a reduction in the amount of losses. Mint is also mentioned as a control crop, but in my own trial didn't work very well. Dispose of carrots affected by root fly by burying them in a deep hole, 30cm (12in), in the garden, rather than putting them on the compost heap. *Slugs* will attack emerging carrot seedlings; use slug traps until carrots are big enough, about pencil thickness. *Rabbits* will attack at all stages of growth; nets are the only way of dealing with them. *Aphids* can do a lot of damage, directly by sucking sap from the leaves, but also by spreading viruses; use a washing-up liquid and water spray to control them as soon as noticed.

HARVESTING

Time from sowing to first harvest: 12 weeks. Can be harvested as soon as they are 1–2cm (½in) in diameter. Can be harvested directly out of the ground over winter.

When to harvest: about pencil thickness to start with, then use as required.

Storing: carrots can be lifted in the autumn and stored in moss peat or sand in a container in a frost-proof and rat-proof shed. Twist off the leaves. They should not be washed. Do not store split or damaged or diseased carrots. In mild areas, they can be left in the ground. In cold areas you could also leave in the ground, but cover with straw or old newspapers.

Good points: Very popular crop. Wide range of varieties and types, mostly winter-hardy.

Bad points: Very susceptible to weed competition. Susceptible to carrot-root fly. Seedlings susceptible to slugs. Rabbits love them.

DO

- Sow thinly.
- Sow 1–2cm (½in) deep.
- Sow in deep, well-prepared soil.
- Choose a sunny aspect.
- Prepare the soil well.
- Keep free of weeds.
- Take precautions against attack by rabbits.
- Grow early crops under fleece or plastic sheets or cold frames.

DON'T

- Sow where carrots or parsnips were sown in the previous three years.
- Sow before early March.
- Sow seed thickly.
- Sow in heavy soils.
- Leave thinnings lying around the ground.

CAULIFLOWER

A member of the brassica (cabbage) family. There are varieties for each season and all are treated differently. Can be temperamental to grow. All cauliflowers can be sown directly into ground or transplanted from a seedbed or seed tray. The bolting or running to seed in cauliflower is referred to as 'buttoning'. The late summer/autumn types are not as prone to buttoning as the summer types, so these are best for beginners.

(summer cauliflower)

*MEDIUM

Summer cauliflower is a small type with a small frame and curd. It is very prone to buttoning (premature running to seed). By using bought-in plants there is a risk that the plants may not have been treated properly to prevent buttoning. Raising the plants is difficult as minimum temperatures must be maintained until plants are hardened off. Varieties are the same as early summer cauliflower, but the time of sowing makes the difference.

HOW TO GROW
Seeds
Earliest time to sow: *indoors* March.
Latest time to sow: early May.
Best time to sow: *indoors* or *outdoors* April.

Depth of sowing: 1cm (½in).

Germination time: 14–21 days.

Lifespan of seeds: 3–5 years.

Successional sowings: sow every 2–3 weeks in small quantities, in sowing period.

Plants

Earliest time to plant: mid- to late April.

Latest time to plant: early June.

Best time to plant: May.

Stage of growth: at 2–3 rough-leaf stage.

Best aspect: southerly and well-sheltered.

Best soil: well-drained, rich, light to medium loam.

Soil preparation: dig deep and mix in manure and compost; seedbed needs to be very well prepared and free of stones and clods. Manure is not needed in seedbed.

Space between plants: 30cm (12in).

Distance between rows: 45cm (18in).

Depth of planting: to soil mark on stem.

Growing situations: raised beds, drills or on the flat.

Best varieties: Early London, White Top, Early Snowball.

MANAGEMENT

- Protect from rabbits and pigeons with netting.
- Earth-up around plants 3–4 weeks after planting out.
- Put out slug traps from the seedbed stage onwards.
- Monitor plants for aphids and caterpillars, and take control measures.
- Bend the leaf over the curd as soon as it appears to prevent it going brown and tough in the sunlight.

PESTS AND DISEASES

See Cabbage p72.

HARVESTING

Time from sowing to harvest: 12 weeks.

When to harvest: should be harvested when curd is a reasonable size, 10–14cm. Don't let the curd get brown.

Storing: don't store. Not good for freezing. Will go off rapidly in heat.

Good points: Small heads, close spacing. Responds very quickly to feeding.

Bad points: Very susceptible to buttoning (running to seed). Can be damaged by a late frost. Very attractive to pigeons and rabbits.

DO

- Pick a good variety.
- Plant in good rich soil.
- Prepare soil well.
- Protect against pests.

DON'T

- Plant too late.
- Plant too close together.
- Plant in poor soil.

(late summer/autumn cauliflower)

*EASY

HOW TO GROW

Seeds

Earliest time to sow: *indoors and outdoors* early April.

Latest time to sow: end of May.

Best time to sow: May.

Depth of sowing: 1cm (½in).

Germination time: 10–12 days.

Lifespan of seeds: 5 years.

Successional sowing: one sowing is usually enough; you might make 2–3 transplantings.

Plants

Earliest time to plant: early June.

Latest time to plant: late July.

Best time to plant: end June.

Stage of growth: at 2–3 rough-leaf stage.

Best aspect: southerly.

Best soil: well-drained, rich, medium loam.

Soil preparation: dig to clear perennial weeds, and incorporate manure and compost.

Space between plants: 30cm (12in).

Distance between rows: 45cm (18in).

Depth of planting: to soil mark on stem.

Growing situations: raised beds, drills or on the flat.

Best varieties: White Rock, Dok Elgon, Serrano.

MANAGEMENT

- Use nets to protect from rabbits and pigeons.
- Earth-up 4 weeks after planting out.
- Keep weeds under control.
- Slug traps should be put down in damp weather.
- Aphids should be monitored and sprayed with a washing-up liquid and water mix.
- Caterpillars should be monitored and controlled by picking off at juvenile stage.

PESTS AND DISEASES

See Cabbage p72.

HARVESTING

Time from sowing to harvest: 3–4 months.

When to harvest: when curd is large enough but before it turns yellow or brown.

Good points: Reliable cropper. Produces large head.

Bad point: Needs a lot of space to grow.

DO

- Sow the right variety.
- Plant in good, well-prepared soil.
- Protect from pests, slugs, aphids and caterpillars.
- Give plenty space to develop.

DON'T

- Plant into poor soil.
- Plant too close together.
- Allow pests to take over.

CELERIAC

*MODERATELY DIFFICULT

Celeriac is a turnip-rooted celery, a biennial that is not winter hardy. It can be cooked, or grated and used in salads. It has become very popular in recent years and, while not the easiest crop to grow successfully, it can be made simpler by following a few basic rules.

HOW TO GROW

Seed must be sown in compost in a seed tray under glass or in a polytunnel.

Seeds

Earliest time to sow: end of February.

Latest time to sow: early April.

Best time to sow: March.

Depth of sowing: on the surface of compost.

Germination time: 14 days.

Lifespan of seeds: 5 years.

Successional sowings: one sowing.

Plants

Earliest time to plant: early April.

Latest time to plant: end of May.

Best time to plant: May.

Stage of growth: 3–4 rough-leaf stage.

Best aspect: southerly.

Best soil: deep, well-drained but moisture-retentive, rich soil.

Crop will be small if planted in poor soil.

Soil preparation: dig deep, eliminate perennial weeds and incorporate manure and compost.

Space between plants: 30cm (12in).

Distance between rows: 45cm (18in).

Depth of planting: ensure bulb is just above soil level.

Growing situations: raised beds, drills or on the flat.

Best varieties: Alabaster, Monarch.

MANAGEMENT

- Harden-off before planting out.
- Water in dry weather as bolting often follows a dry spell.
- Keep weeds under control.

PESTS AND DISEASES

Pests: *Slugs* are a problem for celery throughout its life so keep slug traps in use. *Carrot-root fly* can attack, but good rotation practices will deal effectively with this pest. *Rabbits* will graze on the young plants and netting is advisable.

Diseases: *Celery leaf spot* can be a serious challenge during a wet year; many growers use Burgundy Mixture (see p38) a number of times during the growing season, but I don't use it in the interest of being chemical-free. Instead, I pluck off any leaves with the spot instantly; though some people say it has already gone too far, I have found it helpful.

HARVESTING

Time from sowing to harvest: 6 months.

When to harvest: usually October/November.

Storing: can be stored over winter in a frost-proof store up to late spring. Clean soil off roots before storing. Can also be left in the ground in mild areas, but watch out for frost.

Good point: Will grow in a wide range of soils.

Bad points: Not fully frost hardy. Difficult to propagate from seed. Tiny seedlings need to be pricked out.

DO

- Plant on time.
- Plant in suitable soil.
- Protect from pests and diseases.

DON'T

- Allow plants to dry out.
- Plant too early.
- Plant in a very dry soil.
- Allow weeds to grow over crop.

***TOP TIP

Celeriac seed needs light for germination and is sown on the surface of the moist compost in a temperature of 12°C (65°F).

CELERY

*DIFFICULT

Celery is a member of the carrot (umbelliferae) family and is subject to attack by the carrot-root fly. It is a difficult crop to grow as it requires a soil that retains moisture even in very dry periods. Trench celery, to which it is closely related, is no longer grown in Ireland except for a few dedicated followers, as it is quite troublesome. Bought-in plants may not be properly hardened-off and may bolt.

HOW TO GROW

Seeds

Earliest time to sow: mid-March. Seed must be sown in glasshouse in heat.

Latest time to sow: mid-April.

Best time to sow: late March.

Depth of sowing: leave seed uncovered – just press into moist, peat-based compost rather than a soil or sand-based compost as this is the natural habitat of celery.

Temperature for germination: 11°–12°C (60°–65°F).

Germination time: 18–21 days.

Lifespan of seed: 5 years.

Prick-out: at first rough-leaf stage to 5cm (2in) apart.

Harden-off: over 7–10 days after pricking-out.

Successional sowings: 2–3 sowings, 3–4 weeks apart.

Plants

Earliest time to plant: end May after hardening-off.

Latest time to plant: end June.

Stage of growth: 5–6 rough-leaf stage.

Best aspect: southerly, but well-sheltered.

Best soil: well-drained, but moisture-retaining, medium rich loam.

Soil preparation: dig deep and eliminate perennial weeds. Add in manure and compost and mix well.

Space between plants: 24–30cm (10–12in).

Distance between rows: 30cm (12in).

Special: plant in a square-bed fashion rather than single rows to encourage blanching as they block the light from one another. Some gardeners wrap them, but I don't think it's worth it.

Depth of planting: plant at soil level.

Growing situations: raised beds, drills, on the flat.

Best varieties: Jason, Celebrity, Golden Self-Blanching.

MANAGEMENT

* Celery is a member of the Umbelliferae family, same as carrots and parsnips. Do not plant in same plot where these were grown in previous 4 years.
* Never allow celery to dry out at seedling stage, and try to keep the temperature even, as bolting is caused by uneven or low temperature during the propagation or juvenile stage of the plant.
* Protect from slugs at seedling stage, using slug traps.
* Constant hoeing and hand weeding is needed until plants get too close to each other to do this.

PESTS AND DISEASES

See Celeriac p95.

HARVESTING

Time from sowing to harvest: about 6 months.

When to harvest: when they feel solid and firm; usually end July/early August.

Latest harvest: mid-October or at first severe frost.

How to harvest: harvesting is done by sticking a long, sharp knife into the base of the plant, severing the root and pulling up. Trim the remaining roots off. Dispose of the trimmings in the compost heap.

Good points: Can be grown without trenching. No need to earth up. Neat and clean to harvest.

Bad points: Tends to bolt easily. Not frost hardy. Difficult to grow from seed.

DO

- Grow a self-blanching type.
- Grow in a suitable soil – rich, moisture-retaining loam.
- Get plants from a reliable source.
- Keep soil moist during growing season.

DON'T

- Plant in dry soil.
- Allow to dry out in growing season.
- Allow weeds to get out of control.

***TOP TIP

Grow in the most moist part of garden and add as much dung or compost as possible.

COURGETTES

*MODERATELY EASY

Courgettes are actually immature vegetable marrows that have been pollinated. Seeds are big enough to be sown in individual pots. They like a deep, rich soil and plenty of space to develop.

HOW TO GROW

Seeds

Earliest time to sow: *indoors* end of February, *outdoors* mid-April.

Latest time to sow: *indoors* mid-June (for transplanting out or for transplanting indoors); *outdoors* mid-June (for growing outdoors).

Best time to sow: *indoors* March, *outdoors* April.

Depth of sowing: 2cm (1in).

Germination time: 7–10 days.

Lifespan of seeds: 3–5 years.

Successional sowings: one sowing is usually sufficient, but a second sowing of seed outdoors in mid-June will give a crop right up until early October.

Plants

Earliest time to plant: early May when risk of frost is gone.

Latest time to plant: end of June.

Best time to plant: May.

Stage of growth: 2–3 rough-leaf stage, after hardening-off.

Best aspect: southerly and well-sheltered but with air movement.

Best soil: warm, well-drained, rich, medium loam.

Soil preparation: dig a hole 35cm (14in) x 35cm (14in) and 25cm (10in) deep for each plant, and incorporate manure and compost.

Space between plants: allow 1.5 metres (5ft).

Depth of planting: to soil mark on stem.

Growing situations: can be grown in a raised bed or in open ground. My experience is that it does not always do well in a glasshouse or tunnel as it produces too much foliage in proportion to courgettes, and less insect activity means that pollination is less likely to occur.

Best varieties: Zucchini, Golden Zucchini or Aristocrat.

Number of plants needed for good yield: two for average use.

MANAGEMENT

- Harden-off fully before planting out.
- Water in dry weather.
- Feed with liquid feed during summer.
- Weeds are usually not a problem as the courgette out-grows most weeds, but grass and weeds encourage slugs, so the weeds should not be allowed to develop.
- Help pollination by transferring the male flower (with pollen) onto the female flower (with the small courgette at the bottom); pick the male flower and place it in the centre of the female flower.

PESTS AND DISEASES

Pests: *Slugs* are partial to courgette plants from the seedling stage to adult plant; if young plants are severed at ground level, this is usually caused by slugs; use slug traps.

Diseases: *Botrytis* is usually caused by cold, wet weather or lack of balanced fertiliser; use organic tomato liquid feed to reduce the level of nitrogen and increase the level of potassium.

HARVESTING

Time from sowing to harvest: 14–16 weeks. The cropping season is end of June–October.

Expected yield per plant: 12–20 courgettes.

When to harvest: when the fruit is about 15–20cm (6–8in) long and over 3cm (1in) in diameter.

How to harvest: cut off from stem rather than pulling.

Continuous harvesting: pick courgettes as they mature and continue to do so whether they are required for use or not. This encourages further cropping.

Disposal of plant: when the first frosts burn off the leaves, pick the remaining fruits, pull the plant up and put it on the compost heap.

Good points: Easy for the beginner if grown from raised plants rather than from seed. Will cope easily with weeds, as courgettes are rampant growers. Matures fast.

Bad points: Frost-tender when young. Does not like cold, wet weather. Cannot be stored over winter.

DO

• Raise the plants in gentle heat in glasshouse or polytunnel.

• Sow seed 2cm (1in) deep.

• Harden them off or wean them to outdoor temperatures.

• Plant in rich soil.

• Raise individual plants from a seed sown in compost in 7–8cm (3in) pot.

• Give plenty of space, as much as 3sq metres (150cm x 150cm) (3sq yards).

• Prepare the ground well by deep digging, 27–30cm (10–12in).

• Choose a sunny situation.

• Provide protection against slugs.

DON'T

• Sow seeds too close together, minimum 5cm (2in) apart.

• Plant out until danger of frost is over.

• Leave short of water in warm weather.

• Allow mature courgettes to remain on plant.

• Grow in glasshouse or polytunnel as it will grow too rampant.

***TOP TIP

In cold, wet weather, when there is little bee activity and no pollination, pick off the male flower and push it into the female flower (the one with the miniature courgette on it – this will drop off and rot if not fertilised). Leave it there and usually there is another male flower ready to do the same the following week. Remember – no pollination, no courgette.

CUCUMBER

*MEDIUM

Cucumbers are normally associated with glasshouses, but good crops of excellent flavour can be got from outdoor crops, especially if a cloche or cold frame is used in cold weather. They like a warm, sheltered situation with a free-draining, rich soil.

HOW TO GROW

Seeds

Earliest time to sow: *indoors* mid-March; *outdoors* end of April.

Latest time to sow: *indoors* end of May; *outdoors* mid-June.

Best time to sow: *indoors* April, *outdoors* May.

Depth of sowing: 1cm (½in) deep in small pots (one seed per pot).

Germination time: *indoors* 6–7 days; *outdoors* 9–10 days.

Lifespan of seeds: 5–6 years.

Successional sowings: 2–3 sowings.

Plants

Earliest time to plant: April.

Latest time to plant: mid-June.

Best time to plant: May.

Stage of growth: 2–3 rough-leaf stage, when plants are hardened-off.

Best aspect: sheltered, southerly site.

Best soil: a very rich, deep, well-drained soil, well supplied with dung or compost.

Soil preparation: dig deep, remove perennial weeds and add manure or compost.

Space between plants: 45–60cm (18–24in).

Depth of planting: to soil mark on stem.

Growing situations: raised beds, drills or on the flat.

Best varieties: Burpee Hybrid, Marion, Zeppelin.

MANAGEMENT

- Pinch-out growing point when plant is about 20–25cm (8–10in) high to force plant to branch out into 2 or 3 shoots.
- Help pollination by putting male flower into the female flower (there's a miniature cucumber on the stem underneath the female flower).
- If grown inside, train up on a string or cane.
- Water regularly.
- Give liquid feed as cucumbers develop.
- Keep weeds under control.

PESTS AND DISEASES

Pests: *Slugs* can attack small plants and developing fruits in wet weather; put out traps on time.

Diseases: *Botrytis* can affect both the blossoms and the small cucumbers. Always ensure a balanced feed is given as a top dressing, eg don't over-use nettle feed, and balance it with seaweed feed.

HARVESTING

Time from sowng to harvest: usually early August onwards until first frosts.

When to harvest: before they become over-mature and lose their juiciness; better under-mature than over-mature.

How to harvest: the cucumbers should be cut off rather than pulled off.

Good points: Can be grown in a cold frame as well as polytunnel and glasshouse. During a warm summer can grow outside.

Bad points: Very dependent on warm weather.

DO

- Plant in a rich soil and in a warm situation.

DON'T

- Neglect weed or pest (pigeons) control.

***TOP TIP

Harvest whether needed or not to encourage further growth.

FENNEL

*DIFFICULT

More a luxury than mainstream in Ireland, fennel is a member of the Umbelliferae (carrot) family. Because of its tendency to bolt, it is not often grown. Don't plant where carrots or parsnips have grown in previous 3–4 years.

HOW TO GROW

Seeds

Earliest time to sow: *indoors* and *outdoors* early June; thin-out.

Latest time to sow: *outside* for direct growing (no transplanting) end of June.

Best time to sow: mid-June.

Depth of sowing: 1cm (½in).

Germination time: 18 days under glass, 21 days outdoors.

Lifespan of seeds: 5 years.

Successional sowings: one sowing.

Plants

Earliest time to plant: early June.

Latest time to plant: end June.

Best time to plant: mid-June.

Stage of growth: third rough-leaf stage.

Best aspect: a southerly, well-sheltered aspect.

Best soil: a deep, well-prepared, rich, light medium loam.

Soil preparation: dig deep to eliminate perennial weeds and incorporate manure and compost.

Space between plants: 25–30cm (10–12in).

Distance between rows: 45cm (18in).

Depth of planting: to soil mark on stem – don't bury too deep.

Growing situations: raised beds, drills, on the flat.

Best varieties: Zefa Fina, Rudy, Trieste (all for direct sowing, not transplanting); Selma Fino (reputed to be bolt-resistant, though I haven't tried it yet).

MANAGEMENT

- Never allow plants to dry out.
- Protect from slugs.

PESTS AND DISEASES

Remarkably free of these.

HARVESTING

Time from sowing to harvest: 4–5 months.

When to harvest: when bulb is well formed.

Good points: An unusual vegetable, worth exploring for its interesting flavour. Very few pests and diseases.

Bad points: Bolts very easily. Seedlings susceptible to slug damage.

DO

- Grow in rich soil.
- Sow seed in warm conditions.
- Keep weeds under control.
- Give plenty space to develop.

DON'T

- Sow too early.
- Grow in a cold area.
- Transplant mature plants.

GARLIC

*EASY

A perennial bulb of the onion family that grows underground as distinct from most onions, which have bulbs overground. The leaves are keeled, unlike the onions that are cylindrical.

HOW TO GROW

Grown from bulbs or cloves, outdoors. Get bulbs from garden centre or supermarket and divide up into small cloves (bulbils). Bulbs originating in China are superior to those from Italy or North Africa because of climate.

Bulbs

Earliest time to plant: November; this usually gives a better and earlier crop than spring-planted bulbs.

Latest time to plant: March.

Best time to plant: early December.

Successional plantings: not more than two are necessary, one in autumn and another in spring.

Best aspect: south, with good shelter.

Best soil: deep, well-drained, medium to light loam

Soil preparation: eliminate perennial weeds; add in manure and/or compost and mix well with soil.

Space between bulbs: 15–20cm (6–8in).

Distance between rows: 45cm (18in).

Depth of planting: 5–7cm (2–3in).

Growing situations: drills, on the flat, raised beds, containers.

Best varieties: whatever's available.

MANAGEMENT

- Keep free of weeds.
- Water in dry weather.
- Harvest and lift as foliage withers.

PESTS AND DISEASES

Pests: No serious pests.

Diseases: As it is a member of the onion (Allium) family, it is subject to *white rot*, and as the bulbs may carry some disease on the roots it is advisable to remove the loose outer skin off the mother bulb (bulb from which the small bulbils or cloves are obtained) before planting.

HARVESTING

Time from planting to harvest: autumn planting 7–8 months; spring planting 5–6 months.

When to harvest: when leaves have died down completely.

How to harvest: dig up the bulbs, shake the soil from them and leave in a dry, airy situation to dry. After 7–10 days, clean off the outer skin and pull off the stems before leaving in a dry storage place.

Good points: Winter hardy. Very few pests and diseases.

Bad points: Long growing season. Hard to dry.

DO

- Plant in well-prepared ground.
- Water in dry weather.

- Harvest when foliage starts to wither.

DON'T

- Plant too late.
- Plant too deeply.
- Plant in poorly drained, wet soil.

JERUSALEM ARTICHOKES

*EASY

Best known for their knobbly, badly shaped tubers and also for the height of the foliage, often reaching 1.8 metres (6ft) or more. Sometimes used in cooking as an alternative to potatoes. They form a kind of hedge and are sometimes used as a screening plant against wind.

HOW TO GROW

These are grown from tubers, usually available at good garden centres in spring (though often passed around between gardeners). Those available at supermarkets or greengrocers for cooking are quite suitable to grow in garden. Sprout as for potatoes in January and February.

Tubers

Best time to plant: February/March, when sprouted.

Latest time to plant: end April.

Best time to plant: April.

Best aspect: south.

Best soil: deep, well-drained, medium loam.

Soil preparation: add manure or compost if soil is not rich.

Space between plants: 45cm (18in).

Distance between rows: 45cm (18in).

Depth of planting: 15–18 cm (6–7 in).

Growing situations: open ground, containers.

Best varieties: Boston Red, Fuseau.

Average yield per plant: 1kg (2–3 lbs).

Number of plants required to give a good yield: about 20.

Life span: these are treated as annuals so you save tubers for the next year.

MANAGEMENT

* Earth-up soil around stems when shoots are 25–30cm (10–12in) high.
* Water during dry spell.
* Gather up all small tubers as these will grow as weeds if left scattered on surface of soil or covered.
* Keep a constant look-out for slugs.

PESTS AND DISEASES

Pests: *Slugs* attack at various stages, and it is essential to try to prevent them getting into tubers as you cannot do anything about them then; put out traps just before earthing-up.

Diseases: Remarkably free of diseases.

HARVESTING

Time from planting to harvest: about 5 months. You can leave them in the ground over winter, unless there is frost.

When to harvest: when foliage dies down.

- When harvested, put leftover stems on compost heap, but cut in two to help breakdown.

Good points: Easy to grow. Provides shelter for other crops. Not subject to many diseases. Easily propagated.

Bad points: Grows tall and causes shading. Very susceptible to slug damage in winter and spring.

DO

- Allow plenty space between rows.
- Add manure or compost before planting.
- Plant in a sheltered, sunny area.
- Allow adequate space between tubers.
- Put discarded foliage on compost heap.

DON'T

- Plant in poorly drained ground.
- Plant too close to other vegetables or fruit.
- Leave in ground over winter.
- Plant too deep.

KALE

*EASY

An extremely hardy type of cabbage with a very curly leaf and strong, cabbage-like flavour. It will survive in cold areas better than ordinary cabbages. Do not plant where brassicas were grown in the previous 4–5 years.

HOW TO GROW

Seeds

Earliest time to sow: *outdoors* first week of May.

Latest time to sow: mid-May.

Best time to sow: early May.

Depth of sowing: 1cm (½in).

Germination time: 10–12 days.

Lifespan of seeds: 5–6 years.

Successional sowings: one sowing and one transplanting.

Plants

Earliest time to plant: first week of July.

Latest time to plant: end of July.

Best time to plant: mid-July.

Stage of growth: 2–3 rough-leaf stage.

Best aspect: southerly, with reasonable shelter.

Best soil: good, deep, well-drained, rich, medium loam.

Soil preparation: dig deep and incorporate manure and compost.

Space between plants: 30–35cm (12–14in).

Distance between rows: 45cm (18in).

Growing situations: raised beds, drills or on the flat.

Depth of planting: to soil mark on stem.

Best varieties: Thousand Headed, Tall Green, Dwarf Green.

MANAGEMENT

• Earth-up plants 4–6 weeks after planting out.

• Use nets to protect from rabbits and pigeons.

• Monitor slug activity and put out slug traps.

PESTS AND DISEASES

See Cabbage p72.

HARVESTING

Time from sowing to harvest: 6 months.

When to harvest: December to March

How to harvest: pluck off mature leaves as required, starting with the lower leaves.

Good points: Very hardy and frost-resistant. Not affected by many pests or diseases.

Bad point: Long time to mature.

DO

• Sow seed ½in deep.

• Sow seed in early May.

• Transplant in July.

• Allow 30–35cm (12–14in) between plants.

• Allow 45–60cm (18–24in) between rows.

• Plant in a sunny spot.

• Select best plants.

- Plant mid- to end of July.
- Observe rotation rule, as it is a brassica.

DON'T

- Plant into soft, loose ground.
- Plant too late.
- Allow weeds to get out of control.
- Grow where brassicas were grown in previous 3–4 years.

KOHL RABI

*MODERATELY EASY

This is a member of the brassica family and though not very popular in the past is gaining popularity because, though like turnips and swedes, it is regarded as having a better flavour. The crop is interesting in that it is the modified stem that is the edible part and not the root or leaves. Can be grated raw and used in salads or used as a cooked vegetable. It does not like to be transplanted, so it has to be sown where it is to mature, and thinned-out. A great crop to grow.

HOW TO GROW

Seeds

Earliest time to sow: *indoors* mid-March; *outdoors* mid-April.

Latest time to sow: *indoors* or *outdoors* end May.

Best time to sow: early May.

Best aspect: south.

Best soil: deep, well-drained, sandy to light loam.

Soil preparation: dig deep and incorporate manure or compost.

Depth of sowing: 1–2cm (½in).

Space between seeds: sow thinly, 1–2cm (½in) apart.

Germination time: 10 days.

Lifespan of seeds: 4 years.

Thinning-out: thin-out at second rough-leaf stage to 12–18cm (6–8in).

Growing situations: on the flat, drills, raised beds.

Successional sowings: make a sowing every 4 weeks for continuity.

Space between rows: 45cm (18in).

Best varieties: Vienna varieties are good and include Red Vienna, Purple Vienna and Green Vienna. Red and green varieties are better for indoors and early crops. Purple varieties are better for later in season.

Number of plants needed for a good yield: 30–40.

MANAGEMENT

• Thin-out as plants develop.
• Make one early sowing inside and others outside.
• Water in dry weather.

PESTS AND DISEASES

Pests: *Pigeons* and *rabbits* will graze on them at early stages so put up nets as protection. Slugs are a problem from seedling emergence to maturity, so slug traps should be put out.

Aphids usually occur in warm, dry weather, and as soon as the first aphids are seen spray with soft soap or washing-up liquid and water mix. *Caterpillars* will eat the leaves and sometimes eat into the flesh; pick them off by hand or spray them with a solution of salt and water and repeat if necessary.

Diseases: As it is a member of the brassica family it should not be sown where other members of the brassica family were grown in the previous 3–4 years so as to avoid getting *Finger and Toe*.

HARVESTING

Time from sowing to harvest: 5–6 months.

When to harvest: allow the crop to grow to 4–5cm (1.5–2in) diameter but not more than 7–8cm (3in) in diameter. Pull as required.

Storing: they can be stored in a fridge for a few weeks. Kohl Rabi does not store well longterm. Blanch and store in freezer for winter use.

Good point: Grows fast – four months to maturity.

Bad points: They go very tough if not watered in dry weather. Will not grow in cold, wet, heavy or poor soil.

DO

- Sow in rich, warm, well-drained soil.
- Thin-out to correct spacing.
- Thin-out on time.
- Water often in dry weather.

DON'T

- Sow in cold, heavy, poor soil.
- Allow weeds out of control.
- Neglect pest control.

LEEKS

*MEDIUM TO DIFFICULT

Leeks have gained enormous popularity in recent years in Ireland. They are much milder than onions to which they are closely related. But there's no need to store them, just use straight from the garden. The roots of leeks are non fibrous, and, at transplanting, any soil on their roots tends to fall off. For this reason, and to encourage re-rooting, water after planting. Autumn leeks are long and thin, whereas the over-wintered types are short and much thicker. In former times, gardeners earthed-up leeks, but new varieties do not need this.

HOW TO GROW

Seeds

Seeds may be sown in cellular trays or seed trays, or in a seed-bed outside.

Earliest time to sow: *indoors* February; *outdoors* March.

Latest time to sow: *indoors* mid-May (this may overtake the earlier sowings because of heat); *outdoors* end of April.

Best time to sow: *indoors* February–March; *outdoors* March/April.

Depth of sowing: 1–2cm (½in) deep.

Germination time: 3 weeks or longer.

Lifespan of seeds: 2 years.

Successional sowings: 2–3 sowings of early-maturing varieties; one sowing of main crop.

Plants

Earliest time to plant: early June (early varieties); mid-June (late varieties/main crop).

Latest time to plant: end June (early varieties); late June–July (late varieties/main crop).

Best time to plant: early June (early varieties); June/July (late varieties/main crop).

Stage of growth: when plant is at pencil thickness.

Best aspect: southerly or south-westerly.

Best soil: light to medium loam.

Soil preparation: dig deep and incorporate manure and compost prior to planting.

Space between plants: 15–20cm (6–8in)apart.

Distance between rows: 60cm (24in).

Depth of planting: 5–7cm (2–3in) below soil level. Make a hole with a dibber and sit plant into it; water, but do not fill with soil to allow room for the leek to expand.

Growing situations: raised beds, drills or in the flat.

Best varieties: *early*: Jolant and Prelina; *mid-season*: Argenta, Musselburg, Longina; *late*: Blizzard, Cortina.

MANAGEMENT

Weed control is vital at all stages.

Water and feed in dry weather.

PESTS AND DISEASES

Pests: No serious pests.

Diseases: Rust can be serious if rotation is not practised.

HARVESTING

Time from sowing to harvest: 6–7 months for early crops and 8 months for main crop.

When to harvest: when they are about 2.5cm (1in) in diameter; delayed harvesting will cause leeks to run to seed and become tough and useless.

How to harvest: dig up with a spade or fork and shake soil off roots; then cut roots clean off near the base of the stem.

Storing: leave in the ground over winter.

Good points: Mostly pest- and disease-free. Winter hardy varieties available. Can be sown directly into ground and thinned-out.

Bad points: Very long growing season. Hard to harvest.

DO

- Sow and transplant on time.
- Choose a rich, deep soil.
- Control weeds.

DON'T

- Sow late.
- Transplant late.
- Plant in poor soil.
- Neglect weed control.

Leeks have summer/autumn and winter varieties. Plant, sow and harvest the varieties in their intended season.

LETTUCE
and other salad leaves

*EASY

This is the most popular of all crops grown by beginners and experienced gardeners alike. Lettuces of all sorts are rewarding to grow. In general, they have few demands and their requirements are easily met. It is an easy crop to grow in a warm summer, and can be grown outside, in raised beds, or containers. But it is not easy early in the year in the Irish climate; it is then best grown in a glasshouse or polytunnel, or covered by a cloche or cold frame.

Lettuce should be a priority for the home garden as the leaves are eaten fresh. You can grow your favourite types and make up your own mix. Above all, you will know that there is no contamination from chemicals or additives.

Of all the crops that need successional sowings, lettuce certainly should be sown frequently, even as close as every 7–10 days in warm weather. The best guide is to make another sowing when the previous one has germinated.

Included in this section, are sowings of salad leaves of all types – rocket, chicory, endive and other leaves. Some plants we are treating here as 'lettuce' are not true lettuces botanically, but are grown and eaten as lettuces. Most of these non-true lettuces suffer the big disadvantage that they go to seed very fast in our climate. They also prefer not to be moved, so it is best to sow the seed where the plants are to grow and mature; they can be thinned-out, but, unlike true lettuces, the thinnings are discarded.

LETTUCE VARIETIES

There are four main types of lettuce: Cos, Crisp, Butterhead and Looseleaf. When I first started to grow, the most popular was butterhead, then the preference changed to the crisp types, which are now being challenged by the looseleaf types. Cos is rarely grown now.

BUTTERHEAD VARIETIES:

These are yellow-green in colour and form a heart which is soft to touch. They are more tolerant of poor soil conditions than other types. They grow fast, but tend to run to seed fast also.

Best varieties: All the Year Round, Tom Thumb, Avondefiance; Imperial Winter and Arctic King are two varieties suitable for overwintering in mild areas.

CRISP VARIETIES:

Crisp varieties require higher levels of soil fertility and warmer conditions. They are slow to bolt.

Best varieties: Webb's Wonderful, Great Lakes, Saladin.

LOOSELEAF VARIETIES:

These are the easiest lettuces to grow, and, as the group name implies, they do not form compact heads. The leaves are harvested from the lengthening stem as they mature. There is a great array of leaf shapes, sizes, forms and colours, as well as flavours and textures.

Best varieties: Lollo Rosso – a very attractive pink-bronze frilled edge with a small, loose head; Lollo Biondo – a green version of Lollo Rosso; Salad Bowl – deep, delicately lobed, lime green, tender, and very resistant to bolting; Oak Leaf – thin, delicate, soft leaves with good resistance to bolting; Royal Oak Leaf – a darker green than Oak Leaf and holding its colour better on maturing; Red Fire – with red, ruffle-edged leaves, and good resistance to bolting; Tango – bright green, deeply cut leaves, compact, but poor flavour; Simpson Elite – a quick-growing, bright green, crisp, juicy variety, with a highly frilled edge.

Types of plants used as salads but not true lettuces:

Arugula, which is better known as rocket, is grown in the same way as lettuce – sown outside at regular intervals (every 12–14 days) and thinned-out, but not transplanted.

Mache (Corn Salad or Lamb's Lettuce).

Mizuna (an Asian variety of Mustard Green).

- **The planting instructions given here apply to all of the above salad plants. They will vary in their life span, some lasting only a week, others far longer. It is vital, also, to follow the instructions on the seed packet as these are specific to that variety. The most important thing to remember is successional sowing to achieve continuity of supply.**

HOW TO GROW

Seeds

Lettuce seed can be sown in seed trays or cellular trays and planted out after hardening-off; it can be sown and grown outdoors; it can be sown and grown indoors. Sow seed very thinly and, while thinning-out may be necessary, the thinnings can be transplanted. Sow only a small quantity each time, otherwise there will be waste of seed and waste of effort.

Best place in crop rotation: after a well-manured crop, like potatoes or cabbage.

Earliest time to sow: *indoors* February; *outdoors* April.

Latest time to sow: *indoors* early September; *outdoors* mid-July.

Best time to sow: *indoors* March, *outdoors* May.

Depth of sowing: 1–2cm (½in).

Germination time: 10–12 days.

Lifespan of seeds: 3 years.

Successional sowings: every 7–14 days.

Plants

Indoors and outdoors – control over environment indoors means that planting times are not too specific and depend on the stage of development of the plant rather than on the weather. Transplanting applies only to true lettuces; do not transplant the non-true lettuces, thin-out instead.

Earliest time to plant: *inside* when plants are 2–3 rough-leaf stage; *outside* April.

Latest time to plant: *outdoors* end of July.

Best time to plant: *outdoors* May.

Stage of growth: second rough-leaf stage.

Best aspect: any aspect except northerly.

Best soil: well-drained, deep, rich, medium to light loam.

Soil preparation: dig deep and incorporate manure and compost. Make sure the soil is not acidic (soil test) as lettuce will not grow in acid soil. Also, if the soil is too hard or sticky, the roots cannot penetrate.

Space between plants: 30cm (12in).

Distance between rows: 30–45cm (12–18in).

Depth of planting: to soil mark on stem.

Growing situations: raised beds are ideal for growing lettuce; can be grown on the flat, in drills, in containers.

MANAGEMENT

- Lettuce likes a nice, even temperature; if growing inside, ventilate when it gets too hot. Too high a temperature or too low a temperature can cause bolting.

- Water frequently in dry weather. Shortage of water can also cause bolting.

- Weed with hoe and hand-weed.

PESTS AND DISEASES.

Pests: *Rabbits* will eat lettuce, and nets are the answer. *Slugs* will eat lettuce at all stages and could wipe out a crop if control measures are not taken on time; use slug traps. *Aphids* will attack in warm, dry weather; spray with a washing-up liquid and water mix. *Cut-worms* and *leatherjackets* will cut the plants at or below ground level; impossible to prevent as they live in the ground from previous crops – however, you can eat the leaves as they only attack the stem.

Diseases: *Botrytis* is the main disease. This is favoured by cool, damp conditions and by excessively high levels of nitrogen in the soil; provide as much ventilation as possible, and lift and discard lettuce gone past its usefulness as Botrytis will thrive on this.

HARVESTING

Time from sowing to harvest: huge variation, depending on the variety; 6–16 weeks on average.

When to harvest: the useful life of a lettuce will spread over a period of time, depending on the variety and the weather; this can vary from 12 days in summer to 6 weeks in winter. The time for bolting is far shorter in warm weather. To check for bolting, feel the top of the head; if it is becoming pointed, the plant is about to bolt – pull up immediately and eat. If a crop is beginning to go to seed, it's best to harvest the whole crop to prevent spread of disease or pests – you might make soup with the extras, give to friends, or put on the compost heap!

How to harvest: with lettuce that forms heads, pull up the whole plant, roots and all; do not cut. Throw waste leaves and root on the compost heap. For cut-and-come types, pluck off the older leaves.

Good points: Fast-growing. Great choice of varieties and types. Can be grown inside or under protection.

Bad points: Very susceptible to slugs. Subject to frost damage in early spring.

DO

- Sow seeds under protection, indoors and outdoors.
- Sow in well-prepared, rich soil.
- Use ready-raised plants for early crops.
- Protect from slugs.
- Make several sowings/plantings throughout the year.

DON'T

- Sow too early.
- Allow weeds get out of control.
- Neglect slug control.
- Grow in lime-deficient soil.

***TOP TIP

Everybody will have their own likes and dislikes, and buying a packet of mixed varieties is often a good idea, and can throw up new and sometimes interesting tastes. Where it is felt that this mix does not offer enough of a particular type, for example Crisp, then adding in a few seeds of a crisp type with the other seeds will produce the right mix.

ONIONS

There are many types of onion grown in the garden. Some are grown from seed to produce bulbs and scallions; others are grown from miniature onion bulbs (sets) to produce big bulbs; shallots (see p156) multiply to give up to five or eight bulbs. The onions in each of those categories can be coloured red or yellowish brown. They are all subject to a soil-borne disease called *white rot*, so never plant or sow onions where they were grown in the previous three to four years.

The bulbing process in onions commences in early June and the size of the bulb will depend on the number and size of the leaves at that time. The more leaves and the larger they are, the bigger the bulb. The size of the bulb is also influenced by how close together the bulbs or plants are. The ideal plant density is 8 plants (bulbs) per 30sq cm (1sq ft). Where large-sized bulbs are required, give more space.

(onions grown from seed)

*DIFFICULT

HOW TO GROW

Seeds

Earliest time to sow: *indoors* end of February in cell trays for transplanting; *outdoors* mid-March in ground where they are to grow on and mature. A fine finish is required for sowing seed. The seedbed should be made firm by walking on it while soil is dry before seed is sown.

Latest time to sow: mid-April.

Best time to sow: end March.

How to sow: sow seed thinly, about 1–2cm (½–¾in) apart for thinning-out. For transplanting, sow 6–8 seeds in each cell tray.

Depth of sowing: 1–2cm (½–¾in).

Germination time: *indoors* 3 weeks; *outdoors* up to 4 weeks.

Lifespan of seeds: 2–3 years.

Successional sowings: one sowing only.

Plants

Earliest time to plant: mid- to end of April after hardening-off.

Latest time to plant: mid-May.

Best time to plant: early May.

Stage of growth: at 1–2 rough-leaf stage. Plant the group of 6–8 plants together as a group to the same depth as in cell. Some or all compost should remain attached to the roots; if all compost falls off roots, then delay the planting.

Best aspect: southerly with shelter.

Best soil: light to medium loam.

Soil preparation: dig out all perennial weeds and large stones greater than 7–10cm (3–4in) before adding in manure or compost. Rake to a fine finish before planting.

Space between plants: thin-out to 3–5cm (1–2in). Transplant clusters (6–8) of plants 24–30cm (10–12in) apart.

Distance between rows: 45cm (18in).

Depth of planting: position so the that future bulb sits on top of the soil.

Growing situations: on the flat, drills, raised beds.

Best varieties: Rhijnsburger, Red Baron, James's Keeping.

MANAGEMENT

- Keep weeds under control.
- Protect from slugs at seedling stage.
- Thin-out at 2–3 rough-leaf stage.

PESTS AND DISEASES

Pests: *Slugs* attack emerging seedlings; put out slug traps. *Rabbits* will attack them for the first 4–6 weeks.

Diseases: *White rot*, which attacks the roots, usually occurs where crops have not been grown in a proper rotation. *Neck Rot* occurs on the stored bulbs where the bulbs have not been dried properly or have been stored in a damp place.

HARVESTING AND DRYING

Time from sowing to harvest: 6 months.

When to harvest: when more than 50 percent of leaves have bent over.

How to harvest:

- Bend over or twist all leaves.
- Pull the onions and leave on ground, with roots turned up (to prevent re-rooting). In continuous rain, lay out in boxes in a shed or some other covered area, in a dry, airy spot.
- When most of the leaves have turned yellow or withered, after a week or ten days, move the onions to a dry, airy shed.

Storing: store in a cool, dry shed in net bags, or tie in bundles of 8–10 and hang up.

Good points: Grows in a wide range of soils. Can be stored over winter.

Bad points: Difficult to dry. Long growing season.

DO

- Sow on time.
- Keep weeds under control.
- Sow to the right depth.

DON'T

- Sow too late.
- Allow weeds out of control.
- Plant or sow too thickly.

***TOP TIP

Never allow onions to become damp or wet after drying as they will start sprouting or will rot.

(onions grown from sets)

*EASY

The easiest way to grow onions is from sets. Sets are small onions that were grown from seed the previous year and were harvested before they reached maturity. They are stored under controlled temperatures before being sold to the public for planting in gardens the following spring. The only risk with them is that if sown too early they may bolt or run to seed.

HOW TO GROW

Sets

Earliest time to plant: mid-March.

Latest time to plant: end of April.

Best time to plant: April.

Depth of planting: press sets 1cm (½in) into the ground.

How to plant: press the set into the ground.

Best aspect: southerly.

Best soil: light to medium loam.

Soil preparation: dig out all perennial weeds and large stones greater than 7–10cm (3–4in) and add manure or compost. Rake to a fine finish and firm-up before planting.

Space between plants: space the sets 4–5cm (1.5–2in).

Distance between rows: 45cm (18in).

Growing situations: on the flat, drills, raised beds.

Best varieties: Red Baron – a good, red-skinned main-crop variety; Rhijnsburger – globe-shaped, a good keeper; Stuttgarter – a flattish, early onion, but not the best keeper; Dutch Red; Dutch White. *Set size*: small sets, 550–650 per kilo (250–300 per lb), are less likely to bolt.

MANAGEMENT

- Keep free of weeds.
- Protect from birds after planting.
- Water in dry weather.
- Twist and bend down the stems as the leaves begin to wither.

PESTS AND DISEASES

See Pests and Diseases for onions from seed p131, except that *slugs* do *not* attack onions grown from sets. *Birds* will pick up the sets in the days immediately after planting; use netting if this problem occurs. Both *white rot* and *neck rot* attack onion sets – as for onions from seed.

HARVESTING

Time from planting to harvest: 6–7 months.

How to harvest:

- Lift the bulbs and turn the roots upwards to help them dry after growth is finished.
- Tie in bundles and hang up in a dry, well-ventilated situation.

Good points: Grows in a wide range of soils. Can be stored over winter.

Bad points: Hard to dry. Risk of carrying *white rot* disease on the roots.

DO

- Plant on time.
- Keep weeds under control.
- Plant to the right depth.

DON'T

- Plant too early.
- Allow weeds out of control.
- Plant too thickly.

(spring onions / scallions)

*EASY TO MODERATE

This is a great favourite with most gardeners for a number of reasons, maybe because they have a short growing season and reach maturity fast or possibly because they don't need to be dried and stored. The seed is sown much thicker than for bulb onions and there is a winter hardy variety available.

HOW TO GROW

Seeds

Seeds are sown where they are to grow – no transplanting.

Earliest time to sow: *indoors/outdoors* late February.

Latest time to sow: *indoors/outdoors* mid-June.

Best time to sow: *indoors/outdoors* April.

Best aspect: southerly with shelter.

Best soil: light to medium, well-drained, rich loam.

Soil preparation: dig out all perennial weeds and large stones greater than 7–10cm (3–4in) before adding in manure or compost. Rake to a fine finish and firm-up before sowing.

Depth of sowing: 1cm (¾in).

Space between seeds: sow seed fairly thickly, less than 1cm (½in) apart.

Distance between rows: 30cm (12in).

Germination time: 21 days.

Lifespan of seeds: 2–3 years.

Thinning-out: if sown thinly enough they won't need thinning-out, they are thinned as you use them.

Growing situations: on the flat, drills, raised beds.

Successional sowings: make sowings every 3–4 weeks up to mid-June. For an overwinter crop: make one sowing in early August; leave in the ground to mature the following spring.

Best varieties: White Lisbon for a summer crop; Winter White Lisbon and Ishikura for overwinter crop.

MANAGEMENT

- Keep weeds under control.
- Protect from slugs.

PESTS AND DISEASES

Remarkably free of these, apart from *slugs* at the very early stages. *Rabbits* will sample them if they visit for other crops.

HARVESTING

Time from sowing to harvest: 4 months.

When to harvest: when they are about pencil thickness but before there is a well-defined bulb.

Good points: Grows in a wide range of soils. Grows fast. Winter-hardy variety available.

Bad points: Goes over-mature fast. Risk of slug damage.

DO

- Plant on time.
- Keep weeds under control.
- Plant to the right depth.
- Make successional sowings.

DON'T

- Plant too early.
- Allow weeds out of control.
- Plant too thickly.

PARSNIPS

*MEDIUM TO DIFFICULT

Difficult in early stages, but very winter-hardy. Related to the carrot family, Umbellifera, so the rules for rotation should be followed to avoid picking up diseases and pests. Parsnips need a deep soil, well tilled. Very susceptible to weed cover when small, but very tough as they mature. Cannot be transplanted.

Lifespan of seed: Important! The lifespan is only 2 years. People often sow stale parsnip seeds and are very disappointed when they don't germinate – you can lose a whole month waiting to see if they will germinate or not. It is essential to check the date on the seed packet.

HOW TO GROW

Seeds

Sow where they are to grow.

Earliest time to sow: early February.

Latest time to sow: end of May.

Best time to sow: March.

Best aspect: south or south-west.

Best soil: well-drained, deep, rich, light to medium loam.

preparation: dig deep, eliminate perennial weeds.
t add manure as it causes forking.

epth of sowing: 2cm (¾–1in).

Space between seeds: 1–2cm (1/2–1in).

Distance between rows: 60cm (2ft).

Germination time: 3–4 weeks.

Lifespan of seeds: 2 years.

Thinning-out: at 1–2 rough-leaf stage, thin-out to 15–20cm
(6–8in). Discard the thinnings.

Growing situations: raised beds, drills or on the flat. Parsnips are best grown outdoors as they are a hardy crop; in a
polytunnel they may produce too many leaves, plus they
occupy a lot of space for a very long time where space is at a
premium.

Successional sowings: 2–3 sowings, about a month to 6
weeks apart.

Best varieties: Avonresister, Offenham, Tender and True,
White Gem. I have had best rust-free results with Avonresister;
but I have also grown the other varieties, and while I did have
some rust, I got much bigger parsnips. I couldn't detect any
difference in taste.

MANAGEMENT

- Protect from rabbits with wire netting.
- Monitor for slugs at seedling stage and use slug traps.
- Weed control: by hoe and by hand until plants are
  established.

PESTS AND DISEASES

Pests: Parsnips are subject to *rabbit* damage, like carrots, and should be netted for protection. *Slugs* will damage the seedlings so put out slug traps. *Carrot-root fly* will attack – make sure there is proper rotation.

Diseases: The only serious disease is *rust*, and the variety Avonresister is resistant to rust.

HARVESTING

Time from sowing to harvest: 6–8 months.

When to harvest: earliest crops should be ready in mid-August; main crop ready September/October.

How to harvest: dig up as required.

Storing: leave in the ground until required – exposure to frost is said to enhance the flavour.

Good points: Very hardy. Can be stored in the ground over winter. Long harvest season. Resistant to all but one or two serious diseases.

Bad points: Has to be sown early. Needs a very deep soil. Long time to mature. Occupies land for a long time. Susceptible to carrot-root fly.

DO

- Sow early.
- Sow approx 1cm–2cm (½in) deep.
- Sow fresh, viable seed.
- Choose a deep soil that is rich and well prepared.
- Thin out on time.

PARSNIPS

.0–25cm (8–10in) apart.

,w in badly prepared ground.

- Sow where carrots, parsnips or celery grew in the previous three or four years.
- Sow in land where perennial weeds are present.
- Sow later than end of May.
- Sow too thickly.

***TOP TIP

To reduce risk of carrot-root fly attack, plant some garlic or French marigolds (about 1 marigold to every 12–14 parsnips, planted at random) beside the rows of parsnips and the strong smell should help keep the carrot fly away.

PEAS
and mangetout

*MODERATELY EASY

Peas are a member of the Leguminosae family (same as beans) and they are a very interesting and delicious crop to grow. There are two main types grown in the home garden (a third type, marrowfats, are grown commercially, but are not really worth growing in small quantities); for standard peas, the seeds are allowed to swell, but in the mangetout type the

pods are harvested before seeds swell (you eat the pod
They are both peas, and are handled in the same way. Where
mangetout peas are desired, make sure the correct variety is
sown.

HOW TO GROW

Peas can be transplanted, or sown where they are to grow. If
you soak the pea seed in water overnight they will germinate
much faster.

Seeds

Earliest time to sow: *indoors* mid-February–early March;
outdoors end of March.

Latest time to sow: end of June.

Best time to sow: May.

Depth of sowing: 5cm (2in).

Distance between seeds: 15–21cm (6–7in).

Germination time: 10 days.

Lifespan of seeds: 2–3 years.

Successional sowings: sow every 3–4 weeks. Main crops are
sown from mid-April. I usually do 3 sowings, one early
sowing, one main crop and the last one using an early variety
again.

Plants

Earliest time to plant: early to mid-April after hardening-off.

Latest time to plant: mid-June.

Best time to plant: May.

Stage of growth: 2–3 rough-leaf stage.

Best aspect: southerly and sheltered.

Best soil: deep, rich, well-drained, medium loam.

(PEA AND MANGETOUT)

on: dig deep, eliminating perennial weeds and
manure and compost.

een plants: 15–20cm (6–7in).

etween rows: 150–180cm (5–6ft); this seems a lot
but it allows light to penetrate when the plants are bigger.

Depth of planting: to soil mark on stem.

Growing situations: raised bed or flat ground (but if grown
in a raised bed they will grow very tall); can be grown in a
polytunnel but may cause a lot of shading for other crops. For
an early crop, start off under protection and transplant out.

Staking: provide support stakes or netting to help plants
climb. You can use bamboo, twigs, wire or plastic mesh, or
netting supported on stakes – it's better to have this up before
planting as less damage is done to the plants. Dwarf types can
be grown without staking, but you get better-developed pods
with staking.

Best varieties: *early crop* Early Onward, Pilot; *main crop*
Onward, Senator, Bikini. *Note*: for late crops, sown at end of
June, the early varieties are used.

Mangetout varieties: Sugar Snap, Sweet Green.

Yield per plant: 200–250gm (6–8oz) per plant.

MANAGEMENT

- Water in dry weather.
- Pick maturing pods whether required or not, to encourage
  further cropping.
- Weeds can be serious at the early seedling stage and should
  be removed as they harbour slugs, which can do a lot of
  damage.

PESTS AND DISEASES

Pests: Control *aphids* on developing pods by spraying with water and washing-up liquid. *Rabbits*, *crows* and *pigeons* are all keen on peas, and netting is necessary. *Slugs* attack the emerging seedlings, so slug traps should be put out.

Diseases: There are numerous root diseases that affect peas and rotation is the only way to avoid them.

HARVESTING

Time from sowing to harvest: 3–4 months.

When to harvest: when peas have swollen in pod. Over-maturity: the pods lose their bright green colour and become slightly wrinkled. The peas themselves lose their sweetness and tenderness.

When to harvest mangetout: harvest at the earlier pod stage when the seeds are just forming inside and the pod is still flat.

Storing: blanch immediately to stop the enzymes change their constitution from sugars to starches; freeze.

Good points: Very tasty vegetable, and pod peas are rarely available commercially nowadays. Several crops possible from multiple sowings. Can be transplanted from seed sown under protection. Leaves ground very rich for next crop.

Bad points: Needs staking and support. Long growing season.

DO

- Sow in a well-prepared, sunny spot.
- Sow seed 5cm (2in) deep.

- Sow in a trench 15–20cm (6–8in) wide.
- Sow seed about 5–7cm (2–3in) apart.
- Soak seed in water before sowing.
- Protect from birds and rabbits.
- Make several sowings at 3–4 week intervals.
- Provide stakes or supports to growing plants.

DON'T

- Neglect staking.
- Sow too deeply.
- Sow too thickly.
- Leave exposed to attack by pests.

***TOP TIP

Peas always grow better and are attacked less by birds if supported by sticks or canes, and plastic or wire netting. (Commercially they are usually not staked and grow in clumps along the ground.)

POTATOES

*EASY

Best-known of all vegetables in Ireland. Easy to grow, but hard to grow well! Crop may be early, mid-season or late. They like a warm, well-drained, rich soil, well supplied with manure or compost. Certified seed should be used, and planted in ground where no potatoes were grown the previous three years. Blight, which is the greatest threat to growing a successful crop, is dependent on humidity and temperature, and normally occurs in warm, showery weather, never in cold or dry weather.

SPROUTING – indoors

Potatoes are grown from sprouted tubers, which can be bought-in as seed potatoes, or sprouted from a previous crop of potatoes saved over the winter. A tuber is a vegetable that is capable of growing on again after being harvested, and all potatoes fit this function – you can eat them or keep them as seed. Farmers of old usually kept the smaller potatoes as 'seed potatoes'. Potatoes bought for eating are not the best to use as they may have some pests or diseases on them that would not be apparent. You might try some you particularly like if seed potatoes of that variety are hard to find, but it's best not to rely on them.

Best time to start sprouting seed potatoes: January and February.

Best conditions for sprouting: frost-proof, temperature about 4°–5°C (40°–41°F), plenty of light, rat-proof. Avoid darkness and high temperatures.

Number of sprouts per tuber: a minimum of one, preferably 2–3.

How to sprout: as soon as seed potatoes are purchased, and this can be from Christmas onwards, they can be sprouted. The potatoes are placed in a single layer in a box or tray in a bright frost-proof and rat-proof place. Sprouting is usually carried out in a shed, glass house, porch, window sill, but not in the open or in darkness, as darkness leads to thin shoots.

Potatoes can be planted without sprouting, but this is not advisable as you get an earlier and better crop from sprouted tubers. If the sprouted tubers are too big, cut the potatoes, ensuring that each section has at least two sprouts. Check occasionally for aphids on developing sprouts and spray if necessary with washing-up liquid and water. Coming near planting time, in March, the seed should be hardened-off by putting them into cooler temperatures before planting-out; but if they're not sprouting, leave them longer in the heat and light.

Planting – indoors or outdoors

Earliest time to plant indoors under glass or plastic: mid-February to end of March.

Earliest time to plant outdoors: after frost danger has receded in early April.

Latest time for planting outdoors: early May.

Best time for planting outdoors: mid-April.

Best aspect: southerly or south westerly, especially for early crops.

Best soil: deep rich, medium loam, well tilled.

Soil preparation: manure and or compost should be added if available.

Space between tubers: 30cm (12in).

Distance between rows: 60cm (24in) to allow enough soil to earth-up.

Depth of planting: 15–20cm (6–8in).

Growing situations: can be grown in raised beds, drills or on the flat; indoors in a glasshouse or polytunnel; in containers.

Rotation of crops: plant in ground where no potatoes were grown in the previous 4 years.

Best varieties: potatoes are divided into early, mid-season and main crops. Early potatoes are exciting to harvest, but are grown largely for their earliness rather than flavour. Mid-season (second earlies) varieties have a better flavour, but are not as good a keeper as the main crop varieties. To get best value for ground space, the earlies should constitute about a quarter of the total area of potatoes.

Early varieties: Home Guard, Sharpe's Express, Duke of York, Pentland Javelin, Arran Pilot.

Mid-season: Great Scot, Wilja, Maris Peer, Catriona, Estima. These are not quite as early as the 'earlies' but not as good keepers as the main crop. These would be part of the ¾ area planted. Many people grow just early or main crops.

Main crop: Golden Wonder, Kerr's Pink, Cara, Cladagh, Rooster, Desiree, Pentland Dell, King Edward.

Blight resistant varieties:

Foliage resistant: *first earlies* – Orla, Premiere; *mid-season*: Cosmos, Nadine; *main crop* – Cara, Romano, Pentland Dell, Pentland Squire, Symfonie, Sarpo Mira, Sarpo Axona, Sante, Konda.

Tuber resistant: *first earlies* – Orla, Calla; *mid-season* – Cosmos, Nicola; *main crop* – Cara, Record, Sarpo Axom, Kondar, Valour, Sante, Sarpo Mira, Lady Balfour, Picasso.

Average yield per stalk: about 1 kilo (2–3lbs).

MANAGEMENT

- Earthing-up is very important in potato growing: it stabilises the stalk, it prevents frost damage to the emerging stalk, it prevents greening of the developing potatoes.
- *Times to earth-up (twice)*:
  – when stalks are 8–10cm (3–4in) tall and growing fast; prevents frost damage.
  – when stalks are 15cm (6in) high; protects against greening.
- Keep weeds under control.
- Blight warnings are given over the media, and many growers spray with Bordeaux or Burgundy mixtures, which are approved by the Department of Agriculture. However, I never spray; I prefer to take my chances. The earlies almost never get blight, but I have occasionally lost some of my main crop. I have now stopped growing British Queens and Kerr's Pinks because they are more susceptible to blight than the other varieties. I now largely concentrate on Golden Wonders and Roosters.

PESTS AND DISEASES

Pests: *Slugs* are the chief pests and can be prevented by slug traps while the stalks are small. Slug traps are of no use when the slugs go down into the tubers, and you can do nothing about this. *Aphids* can cause direct damage by sucking sap from the leaves, and indirect damage by spreading viral diseases. Control by spraying with water and washing-up liquid. *Eelworm* of potatoes is a tiny worm that builds up over a number of years from continuous growing of potatoes until the crop is no longer viable. The worm is visible to the human eye only in June, when it appears as a small, round, lemon- or orange-coloured attachment to the roots. Each of these is capable of producing hundreds of young eelworms that go on to infest any crop of potatoes planted there in the future. Typical symptoms are stalks going yellow and wilting in a fine spell in May/June, or when a stalk of potatoes is pulled there are only small, marble-sized potatoes, but the skin is mature. Rotation is the only preventative.

Diseases: The main and most serious disease is *potato blight*; I find it best to grow varieties that are more resistant. There are other pests and diseases that will occur, and good rotation is the only solution.

Good points: Easy to grow. Will tolerate a wide range of soils.

Bad points: Susceptible to blight. Need fresh ground every year.

HARVESTING

Time from planting to harvest: 4 months for earlies and 5 months for main crops.

When to harvest: when potatoes drop off as stalks are withering.

How to harvest: early potatoes are dug when the tubers are large enough – the tubers should fall off the stalk easily. Main crop potatoes are dug when all stalks have died back and skin of the potato has cured (does not rub off easily). Main crop potatoes must be lifted and stored in the autumn for use throughout the winter and spring.

Storing: store in a cool, dry place that is vermin-proof. They are stored unwashed, though not covered with earth or sand. They could be put in a bin, and the lid put on loosely to allow air to circulate, allowing them to breathe and thus prevent rotting, but keeping out the light (light makes them go green and inedible).

DO

- Use certified seed potatoes.
- Sprout seed.
- Plant in warm, well-manured ground.
- Plant on time.
- Earth-up the drills after stalks emerge.

DON'T

- Use diseased seed.
- Plant in ground where potatoes were grown in last 4–5 years.
- Sow too deep or too shallow.

***TOP TIP

Grow varieties for the season required, early varieties for early season and main crop varieties for later as the flavour is always better.

PUMPKINS

*EASY

Pumpkins are members of the same family as courgettes, marrows and squashes (cucurbita). They are all fleshy-fruited vegetables and vary in size from the small courgette to the huge pumpkin. The seed is big and so also is the plant, and requires plenty room to develop. If space is at a premium, leave out the pumpkin. It can be grown in a large container and left to trail over any hard surface.

HOW TO GROW

Seeds

The best way is to sow single seeds in pots or cellular containers and put into bigger containers as plants grow before hardening-off and planting outside.

Earliest time to sow: *indoors* end of February; *outdoors* mid-April.

Latest time to sow: *indoors* or *outdoors* early June.

Best time to sow: *indoors* or *outdoors* April.

Depth of sowing: 2.5cm (1in).

Germination time: 8–10 days.

Lifespan of seeds: 4 years.

Successional sowings: one sowing is usually sufficient.

Plants

Earliest time to plant: mid-April.

Latest time to plant: end May.

Best time to plant: mid-May.

Stage of growth: 2–3 rough-leaf stage.

Best aspect: southerly

Best soil: deep, well-drained, rich, medium loam.

Soil preparation: dig a hole 35cm (14in) x 35cm (14in) and 25cm (10in) deep and add manure and/or compost to the soil being put back into the hole.

Space between plants: 1.5 metres (5ft).

How to plant: put plant in hole made by a trowel deep enough to take the plant and put the soil firmly around the root, up to soil mark on plant.

Growing situations: on the flat, drills or raised beds. My own experience with pumpkins in a polytunnel was they grew too rampant and took over too much space for the few pumpkins I got in the autumn.

Best varieties: Hundredweight is a variety I have seen do very well. There are many varieties available as seed, but plants have been hard to get in recent years.

MANAGEMENT

- Always harden-off plants.
- Put plants into larger pots if planting out is delayed.
- Water in dry weather.
- Pinch-out top of main growing shoot when it is about 30cm (12in) long.
- Feed with liquid feed (nettle and comfrey leaves in water).
- As pumpkin depends on pollination to develop, it helps in wet weather to transfer the male flower with pollen into the female flower and let the flies and bees do the pollination.

PESTS AND DISEASES

Pests: *Slugs* will attack the young pumpkin plants for the first few weeks and especially in damp weather; put out slug traps at time of planting out. *Pigeons* and *crows* will pull up seeds and young plants that are sown outside; put up nets.

Diseases: *Botrytis* will attack developing pumpkins and usually starts from the rotting flower blossom which should be removed as soon as it is noticed.

HARVESTING

Time from sowing to harvest: about 8 months.

When to harvest: when leaves begin to wither.

How to harvest: pumpkins can be harvested and used before they reach full size, when the colour begins to turn from green to yellow and brown, usually in September. They should be handled carefully as any bruising may start a rotting point.

Storing: can be stored up to the following March or April in a cool, dry place.

Good points: Easy to grow. Few pests and diseases to cope with. Clashes with few other crops in rotation. Easy to store.

Bad points: Takes up a lot of space. Long growing season.

DO

- Grow in a rich soil.
- Sow seed on time.
- Give plenty space to develop.

DON'T

- Sow or plant late.
- Grow in poor soil.
- Allow plants to dry out.
- Plant too closely together.

RADISHES

*EASY

Radish is a fast-growing, small root of the brassica family, used raw in salads. Several sowings need to be made in the year to give continuity, as it matures very fast. There are three types – globe, intermediate and long.

HOW TO GROW

Can be grown indoors or outdoors, from seed. No transplanting.

Seeds

Earliest time to sow: *indoors* February, *outdoors* mid-March.

Latest time to sow: *indoors* and *outdoors* mid-August.

Best time to sow: *indoors* and *outdoors* April.

Best aspect: southerly.

Best soil: well-drained, rich, medium loam.

Soil preparation: dig and make a fine seedbed without adding manure or compost.

Depth of sowing: 1cm (½in).

Space between seeds: 1cm (½in).

Distance between rows: 30cm (12in).

Germination time: 7 days.

Lifespan of seeds: 5 years.

Thinning-out: sow thinly and no thinning will be required.

Growing situations: raised beds, drills, on the flat, containers. Suitable for intercropping (sowing between rows of other vegetables or fruit).

Successional sowings: sow every 3–4 weeks.

Best varieties: Scarlet Globe, French Breakfast. Many other varieties are available, most are successful.

MANAGEMENT

• Keep weeds in check.
• Make successional sowings.

PESTS AND DISEASES

Pests: As radish is a very fast-maturing crop, the only pests that can cause any serious damage are *slugs*; monitor especially as seedlings emerge.

Diseases: Very few, but can suffer from *Boron* deficiency, which causes blackening of the centres; add Borax.

HARVESTING

Time from sowing to harvest: 3–6 weeks.

When to harvest: when radishes are about 2.5cm (1in) or a little more in diameter.

Good points: Very fast to grow. Popular for salads. Will tolerate a wide range of soils. Can be grown in garden, raised beds or in containers. Good crop for beginners.

Bad points: Goes over-mature very fast. Needs to be sown at regular intervals. Goes to seed very fast. Short cropping season. Susceptible to slugs at early stages.

DO

- Sow in a warm, rich, well-prepared soil.
- Sow seed 1cm (½in to ¾in) deep.
- Sow small quantities at a time.
- Make regular sowings every 10–14 days.

DON'T

- Sow in ground where brassicas were grown in the previous three years.
- Sow too thickly or too deeply.
- Transplant.

***TOP TIP

Radish can be used as a test crop for the presence of Boron in the soil. If Boron is lacking, then the centre of the radish will be black or have black spots. This means that other brassicas will also suffer from the same complaint unless Boron is added.

SHALLOTS

*EASY

Shallots are small onions usually 2–3cm (1–1.5in) diameter, oval to globular in shape, and red or yellow in colour. The difference between shallot and onion sets is that the latter produce one large bulb from each small bulb planted, but shallots produce from 4–8 or more shallot bulbs from each bulb planted. Individual, immature shallots may be harvested and used as spring onions before they become too strong – pull out individual plants, leaving the others to grow on.

HOW TO GROW

Source shallot bulbs at garden centres, farmers' markets or from a fellow gardener.

Bulbs

Earliest time to plant: mid-March.

Latest time to plant: late April.

Best time to plant: mid-April.

Best aspect: southerly.

Best soil: light to medium, well-drained, rich loam.

Soil preparation: dig out all perennial weeds and large stones greater than 7–10cm (3–4in) before adding in manure or compost. Rake to a fine finish and firm before planting.

Depth of planting: press into soil to about 2cm (1in) depth.

Space between bulbs: 20–30cm (8–12in).

Distance between rows: 45cm (18in).

Growing situations: on the flat, drills or raised beds.

Successional sowings: usually one planting is sufficient.

Best varieties: Dutch White, Dutch Red.

MANAGEMENT

Regular weeding and watering during dry weather.

PESTS AND DISEASES

Pests: Not significant. (Even the slugs don't particularly like them!)

Diseases: white rot: see onions, p131.

HARVESTING AND DRYING

Time from planting to harvest: 5–6 months.

When to harvest: when more than 50 percent of the leaves have turned yellow and wilted, they should be pulled up and the roots turned up to dry in the sun.

How to harvest: turn over every few days and move to a dry, airy shed where they will not get wet by rain. They can be tied in hanks or in groups of 10–12 and hung up in a dry place to be used over the winter and early spring.

Best points: Grows in a wide range of soils. Can be stored over winter.

Bad points: Hard to dry. Risk of carrying White Rot disease on the roots.

DO

- Plant on time.
- Keep weeds under control.
- Plant to the right depth.

DON'T

- Plant too early.
- Allow weeds out of control.
- Plant too thickly.

***TOP TIP

Keep a few of the smaller shallots each year to plant the following spring. If the majority of the shallots are small, this indicates they have lost their vigour and should be replaced.

SPINACH

*EASY

Spinach is often confused with spinach beet (also called Swiss chard or perpetual spinach – see p168). True spinach, which we are dealing with here, deserves to be a more popular vegetable because, though it is subject to bolting and has a short cropping life, it is very easy to manage and few pests attack it. It also has a distinctive flavour and is full of vitamins and iron.

HOW TO GROW

Can be planted indoors or outdoors, but it runs to seed very fast indoors, so sow seed outdoors and do not transplant.

Seeds

Earliest time to sow: early March.

Latest time to sow: end June.

Best time to sow: May.

Best aspect: southerly.

Best soil: deep, rich medium loam.

Soil preparation: dig in dung or compost before sowing.

Depth of sowing: 2.5cm (1in).

Space between seeds: 1cm (1/2in).

Distance between rows: 30–35cm (12–14in).

Germination time: 2 weeks.

Lifespan of seeds: 4 years.

Thinning-out: thin-out at second rough-leaf stage to 7–8cm (3in) apart.

Growing situations: raised beds, drills or on the flat.

Successional sowings: every 4–5 weeks to end June.

Best varieties: *summer spinach* – Long Standing Round, Victoria; *winter spinach* – Broad-Leaved Prickly, Long-Standing Prickly.

MANAGEMENT

- Keep weeds under control by hand and by hoe.
- Bolting, or running to seed, can be particularly disappointing as all the plants are usually affected. It is mostly caused by a growth issue – any factor that slows down or stops the growth of a crop, such as cold weather, very warm weather, shortage of water, water logging, attack by pest or disease, shortage of nutrients, disturbance by weeding or hoeing. Encourage even growth by watering regularly, and grow in rich soil. Make more frequent sowings.

PESTS AND DISEASES

Pests: *Slugs* can cause damage from the time the seedlings emerge to the mature plant stage, so keep slug traps out during moist, wet weather.

Diseases: *Downy mildew* can destroy a complete sowing of spinach seedlings and developing plants in a short time, especially in cool, damp weather. Ensure good ventilation and thin-out plants on time.

HARVESTING

Time from sowing to harvest: 3 months.

When to harvest: when leaves are sufficiently big and numerous; can harvest each plant many times.

How to harvest: cut or pluck the leaves at ground level, leaving the root undisturbed.

Good points: Very fast grower. Easy to grow in good soil. Very few pests and diseases.

Bad points: Very fast to bolt. Likes rich soil. Short cropping season. Needs very good weed control.

DO

- Sow in deep rich soil.
- Sow in a warm situation.
- Sow thinly.
- Keep moist.
- Grow a bolt-resistant variety.

DON'T

- Sow in cold, exposed situations.
- Sow too early.
- Sow too thickly.

SWEDES

*MEDIUM

Swedes are closely related to turnips and the names are often interchanged. Swedes, however, are regarded as the hardier relation, and in the past were regarded as being fit only for cattle. In present times they have taken on the role of being a health food.

HOW TO GROW

Transplanting is not suitable for swedes. Seeds should be sown where the plant is to grow. Always plant in ground where no brassicas were grown the previous three years.

Seeds

Earliest time to sow: early May.

Latest time to sow: mid-July.

Best time to sow: mid-May.

Best aspect: south or south west.

Best soil: deep, rich, medium loam with a minimum pH 6.5 (soil test).

Soil preparation: dig deep and eliminate perennial weeds before incorporating manure and compost.

Depth of sowing: 1–2cm (½in).

Space between seeds: sow very thinly.

Distance between rows: 45–60cm (18–24in).

Germination time: 7–10 days.

Lifespan of seeds: 5–6 years.

Thinning-out: to 15–20cm (6–8in) when at 2–3 rough-leaf stage.

Growing situations: raised beds, drills or on the flat – drills are better than on the flat.

Successional sowings: make 2–3 sowings per year.

Best varieties: Magres, Tip Top, Acme.

MANAGEMENT

- *Thinning-out*: best done when plants are at second rough-leaf stage.
- Keep free of weeds.

PESTS AND DISEASES

Pests: *Rabbits* and *pigeons* can be a threat to the crop throughout its cropping life; netting is the only satisfactory prevention and control. *Slugs* will attack swedes from seedling emergence right up to maturity, but swedes are most vulnerable at the seedling stage; use slug traps at all times. *Aphids* can be a serious threat during a dry, warm year and crop should be sprayed with water and washing-up liquid as soon as noticed. *Caterpillars* can attack the leaves of the early crops, but can be even more serious on the late crops; pick off or squeeze off the eggs or small caterpillars as soon as noticed, or spray with a solution of salt and water. The *flea beetle* is best controlled by sowing the crop in early May, as the first generation has gone and the second has not emerged.

Diseases: There are various root diseases that are best controlled by good rotational practices. *Downy mildew* on the leaves can cause serious loss in size and texture, making it tough; reduce by thinning out on time, giving good ventilation and keeping weed-free. Also subject to *finger and toe*, and rotation is the only solution. They may suffer a *Boron* deficiency which you'll notice if the centre is brown or black; add Borax for the following year's growth.

HARVESTING

Time from sowing to harvest: 5 months.
When to harvest: when at least 8–9cm (3–4in) in diameter.
Storing: swedes are frost-hardy in most areas and can be left in the ground until needed, or lifted in November and put in a pit or a frost-proof shed; when lifting for storage, do not cut or

clean, pull them up and shake the soil off the roots, otherwise they become dry.

Good points: Very hardy. Easy to grow.

Bad points: Susceptible to *finger and toe* disease.

DO

- Sow thinly.
- Sow seed 1–2cm (1in) deep.
- Sow where no brassicas were sown in previous 3–4 years.
- Give protection from pests, including pigeons.
- Sow in well-drained, well-prepared ground.

DON'T

- Sow too early, not before early May.
- Allow weeds to grow over them.
- Allow pests to damage the seedlings.

***TOP TIP

Sow in early May when danger of flea beetle is lowest.

SWEETCORN

*EASY–MEDIUM

This crop is very dependent on fine summer weather to fill the cobs. It is related to the field crop maize or corn. The corn grows high, as much as 1.8 metres (6ft), and needs a rich soil and a warm, southerly aspect. It is remarkably free of serious diseases and pests, but likes shelter and a well-drained soil.

HOW TO GROW

The seed can be sown inside in pots or trays for transplanting outside after hardening-off. They can also be sown directly outside where they are to mature, but extra seed must be sown to allow for losses during germination.

Seeds

Earliest time to sow: *indoors* April; *outdoors* mid-May.

Latest time to sow: *indoors* early June.

Best time to sow: *indoors* or *outdoors* May.

Depth of sowing: 2.5cm (1in).

Germination time: 10 days.

Lifespan of seeds: 2 years.

Successional sowings: 2 per year, 3–4 weeks between sowings.

Plants

Earliest time to plant: early May, after hardening-off, when risk of frost has gone.

Latest time to plant: end June.

Best time to plant: late May.

Stage of growth: when plants are about 20–25cm (8–10in) high.

Best aspect: southerly.

Best soil: deep, well-drained, light to medium loam.

Soil preparation: dig deep and remove perennial weeds before incorporating manure and compost.

Space between plants: 45cm (18in).

Distance between rows: 45cm (18in).

Depth of planting: to soil mark on stem.

Growing situations: can be grown in raised beds but can grow too high; more suitable for drills, on the flat, in containers; suitable for polytunnels.

Best varieties: Kelvedon Glory, John Innes Hybrid, Golden Bantham.

Yield per plant: one cob per plant.

MANAGEMENT

- Harden-off plants before planting-out.
- Plant in a square pattern rather than a single line to encourage pollination. When the plants are in flower, shake them slightly during the day to shake the pollen onto the tassels. Lack of pollination leads to empty cobs; this is usually caused by cold, wet weather which leads to lack of insect activity and the pollen becoming sticky.
- In warm, dry weather it is important to water plants a few times a week, especially when the cobs are developing.
- Give liquid feed as cobs are swelling.
- Allow only two cobs per plant, at most, to develop; this gives better standard cobs.
- Keep weeds under control.

PESTS AND DISEASES

Remarkably free of pests and diseases, but the tendency will be to grow it in the sunniest position year after year where it will eventually pick up some pest or disease. Best to rotate.

HARVESTING

Time from sowing to harvest: 4 months.

When to harvest: on peeling back the skin, the seed in the cob should be a light yellow colour and should be soft and sweet, but not milky; if too milky or too soft, they are immature – leave to grow a little longer. But once the sweetness goes they are over-mature. Use as soon as possible after picking to ensure sweetness.

How to harvest: cobs can be broken off, but if there's another cob coming on, cut off so as not to damage the plant.

Good points: Grows well in most soils. Quick to germinate. Does not need staking. Not subject to many pests or diseases. Weeds not a problem.

Bad points: Needs a warm summer to develop fully. Cob needs warm weather to be pollinated for development.

DO

• Sow seed on time.
• Harden-off before planting out.
• Plant in rich, well-prepared ground.
• Plant in a block system, not lines, to aid pollination.

DON'T

• Plant too close together.
• Plant in one straight line.

SWISS CHARD (spinach beet/ perpetual spinach)

*EASY

This is a close relation of beetroot, but in this case the leaf is eaten and the root is allowed to remain in the ground; it is also much less likely to bolt, even in a dry spell. It tastes wonderful if stir-fried quickly, and it looks great in a salad bowl. Can be grown indoors and outdoors, but it does well outside, so don't waste tunnel space.

HOW TO GROW

It's best to sow where they are to mature, and thin-out, avoiding transplanting. This helps to stop bolting.

Seeds

Earliest time to sow: *indoors* and *outdoors* early April.

Latest time to sow: mid-June (for winter crops).

Best time to sow: May.

Best aspect: southerly or south westerly.

Best soil: deep, well-drained, fertile, medium loam.

Soil preparation: dig and remove perennial weeds before adding in manure or compost.

Depth of sowing: 2.5cm (1in).

Space between seeds: 2–3cm (1–1½in).

Distance between rows: 45cm (18in).

Germination time: 10–14 days.

Lifespan of seeds: 3 years.

Thinning-out: at 2–4 rough-leaf stage to 20–25cm (10–12in).

Growing situations: raised beds, drills, on the flat.

Successional sowings: make 2–3 sowings in year at 3–4 week intervals.

Best varieties: Spinach Beet, Swiss Chard, Rainbow Chard.

MANAGEMENT

- Thin-out at 2–3 rough-leaf stage.
- Remove weeds by hoe or by hand.
- Water in dry weather.

PESTS AND DISEASES

Pests: *Rabbits* can be kept from spinach by putting up nets. *Slugs* can be a problem from seedling emergence until harvest time; use traps throughout growing time.

HARVESTING

Time from sowing to harvest: 3 months.

When to harvest: when leaves are big enough and plant is growing vigorously.

How to harvest: cut (especially in dry weather) or pluck the leaves at ground level, leaving the roots undisturbed.

Lifespan: will harvest for a full year if sown successionally. Goes to seed in second year of growth, but can be used until new crop is ready.

Good points: Virtually trouble-free vegetable. Easy to grow.

Fast to mature. Grows in a wide range of soils. Easy to harvest and does not go over-mature fast.

Bad points: Very attractive to slugs. Needs to be thinned-out while young.

DO

- Sow in well prepared, rich soil.
- Sow thinly in drills.
- Sow in April.
- Thin-out on time.

DON'T

- Sow too early.
- Allow weeds to grow over crop.
- Sow too thickly.

TOMATOES

*MEDIUM

Tomatoes are a very popular crop with beginners, especially those with a glasshouse or polytunnel. This is justifiable as the taste of home-grown tomatoes is far better than that of shop-bought ones; it's one time when growing your own really pays off. Tomatoes are related to potatoes and these crops should not be planted close to each other as they both get potato blight. Tomatoes can do well outside in a very fine summer, but they should really be considered an indoor crop in Ireland, suited to a glasshouse or polytunnel. Tomatoes are raised from seed every year. Many people buy-in plants rather than growing from seed, but I feel it's worth trying to raise from seed in order to be sure of the variety; it's interesting to exchange plants with friends and grow several varieties.

HOW TO GROW

Sow the seed thinly in a seed tray, using a seed and potting compost. Water well before covering with a sheet of glass or a plastic bag and put in a warm place. Harden-off before planting outside.

Seeds

Earliest time to sow: *indoors* end of February/early March.

Latest time to sow: *indoors* end of March.

Best time to sow: *indoors* early March.

Depth of sowing: 1–2cm (½in).

Germination time: 9–10 days.

Temperature for germination: 12°C (55°F).

Prick-off: 10–14 days after germination into 7.5cm (3in) pots at second rough-leaf stage. Give plants plenty of light.

Lifespan of seeds: 4–5 years.

Successional sowings: one sowing only.

Plants

Earliest time to plant: *indoors* early April; *outdoors* end April.

Latest time to transplant: *indoors or outdoors* end April – early May.

Best time to plant: *indoors and outdoors* April.

Stage of growth: when plants are 20–25cm (8–10in) high.

Best aspect: a southerly aspect with good shelter.

Best soil: a deep, rich, well-drained, medium loam.

Soil preparation: dig deep, remove roots of perennial weeds and incorporate manure and compost.

Space between plants: 45cm (18in).

Distance between rows: 60–90cm (2–2.5ft).

Depth of planting: to soil mark on stem.

Growing situations: raised beds, containers, grow bags, beds, on the flat, but not on drills as water would drain away too fast.

Best varieties: varieties are classified on the basis of type of plant and type of fruit. There are new varieties constantly being developed and it is best to check the seed packet to determine which type it belongs to.

Type of plant:

1 Cordon or indeterminate or single-stem types; must be trained or tied up on a cane, stake or string.

2 Bush or determinate type; several shoots, but never a main stem, remaining low.

3 Dwarf bush, usually cherry. Some of them have a trailing habit, so best to grow them in a fairly tall or high container so they will trail down.

Type of fruit:

1 Round – standard or normal type (eg Moneymaker).

2 Cherry – many small fruits on one truss or stem.

3 Beefsteak – very big tomatoes.

4 Plum – oval or plum-shaped.

5 Marmande – large, but irregular-shaped.

6 Oxheart – cone-shaped fruit.

There is also a great variety in colour – red, orange, yellow, green, stripy, multicoloured and so on.

Choosing a variety: you need to check for growth habit, fruit type, colour; however, there is a huge range available.

Here is a small selection that I have grown successfully:

Ailsa Craig: very good flavour.

Alicante: excellent flavour, green back.

Big Boy: beefsteak type, good flavour.

Currant Red: tiny cherry tomatoes, excellent flavour.

Currant Yellow: like Currant Red, but fruit is yellow.

Gardener's Delight: good flavour, very popular.

Moneymaker: a very popular variety of indeterminate habit; not great flavour in my opinion.

Sun Cherry: very sweet cherry type.

MANAGEMENT

- Water regularly 2–3 times per week in warm weather, giving 7–8 litres (1.5– 2 gallons) per plant per watering. If the soil dries out, the tomato plant stops growing and the crop is either reduced or delayed or blossom will drop off.
- Feed regularly with nettle feed as soon as fruit starts swelling.
- Support with canes or strings. The stems are tied to canes at intervals of 25–30cm (10–12in), or strings are tied from a wire over the plant and attached to the base of the plant's stem. The string is then twisted around the plant as the plant grows.
- The plant should be trained as a single-stemmed plant; all side-shoots in the axis between the main stem and leaf stems should be removed as soon as they are seen. If these are left to grow uncontrolled, they will sap away the energy of the main plant and the fruit will be small and may fail to develop.

- It is also beneficial to spray the tomatoes overhead on very warm days as it helps to lower the temperature and improve conditions for pollination (as it encourages insect activity).

- As the plant gets taller, the lower leaves begin to turn yellow and brown and wither off. It is normal for the old leaves to die off and these should be removed to allow in more air and light, and prevent rotting. Only 3–4 leaves per plant should be taken off at any one time.

- Sometimes tomatoes split when ripening. The main cause of this is shortage of water just before ripening commences; when water is then given to the plants, the fruit begins to swell again and the skin, which had become tough, is unable to expand and splits to cope with the expansion.

PESTS AND DISEASES

Pests: *Slugs* are a problem while they are seedlings and *aphids* later on.

Diseases: *Botrytis* is a problem in cold, wet weather when plants are small. Tomatoes are susceptible to a number of different physiological diseases, and upsets caused by uneven watering, too high or too low temperature, too dry atmosphere, shortage of minor or trace elements, or imbalance of nitrogen to potassium; in this case, feed with a mixture of seaweed or seaweed extract. *Potato blight* is a problem later in the year, especially outside, if there are high temperatures. Blight shows as black patches on the leaves and shortly afterwards the fruit turns black in parts. The fruit remains hard, and is inedible. Many people spray with Burgundy Mixture, However, I don't spray; instead, I simply put the spoilt fruit on the compost heap. I then take preventive measures for the following year by repairing leaks in the roof or elsewhere.

HARVESTING

Time from sowing to harvest: 6 months or more.

Good points: Many varieties. Matures over a long period.
Bad points: Very dependent on fine weather. Susceptible to blight. Hard to train and manage.

DO

- Sow seed on time.
- Plant on time.
- Plant in a sunny aspect.
- Choose a rich soil.
- Train and manage the plants.

DON'T

- Sow or plant too late.
- Plant in a cold situation.

***TOP TIP

If you want to grow a particular variety you must sow the seed and propagate it yourself as that particular variety may not be available as plants in the garden centre.

TURNIPS

*MEDIUM

Turnips are members of the brassica (cabbage) family and are reasonably easy to grow. They also grow fairly quickly and are one of the first root vegetables to mature in June.

HOW TO GROW

Sow seeds outdoors where they are to grow, and thin-out.

Seeds

Earliest time to sow: early April.

Latest time to sow: mid-August.

Best time to sow: early June.

Best aspect: southerly

Best soil: a deep, well-drained, medium loam.

Soil preparation: dig deep and prepare a fine seedbed.

Depth of sowing: 1–2cm (1in).

Space between seeds: sow as thinly as possible, about 1cm (1/2in) apart.

Distance between rows: 45cm (18in).

Germination time: 9–10 days.

Lifespan of seeds: 5 years.

Thinning-out: at 2–3 rough-leaf stage, to 10–15cm (4–6in) apart.

Growing situations: drills, on the flat, raised beds.

Successional sowings: 4–5 sowings per year.

Best varieties: Early Purple Top, Orange Jelly.

MANAGEMENT

- Thin-out at second rough-leaf stage.
- Use nets to keep out rabbits.
- Keep slugs under control.
- Make successional sowings.
- Keep weeds under control.
- Water in dry weather.

PESTS AND DISEASES

Pests: See Swedes p163.

HARVESTING

Time from sowing to harvest: 12–14 weeks – they can be harvested earlier, at about 5cm (2in) in diameter; will get tough if left grow too big.

Storing: leave in the ground until autumn (not winter hardy).

Good points: One of the fastest-maturing crops. Easy to grow. Tolerates a wide range of soils. Many varieties to choose from.

Bad points: Subject to a lot of pests early in life. Goes to seed or bolts fast. Needs several sowings to give continuity. Warm, rich soil needed to give early and rapid growth.

DO

- Sow seed in a well-prepared seedbed.
- Add in manure or compost before sowing seed.
- Sow seed 1cm (½in) deep.
- Sow seed thinly.
- Protect from pests.
- Thin-out.

DON'T

- Sow too early.
- Sow too thickly.
- Sow too deeply.
- Grow in ground where cabbages or other brassicas were grown in the previous three years.

***TOP TIP

Make several early sowings at two-weekly intervals to ensure continuity and prevent failure caused by frost and slugs.

VEGETABLE MARROWS

*MODERATELY EASY

Of the same family as courgettes, the vegetable marrow is a fairly easy annual crop, grown from seed; one or two plants are usually sufficient to give an adequate supply for the average household. It is grown outdoors in a sunny position and given plenty of space to develop. Does not always do well in a glasshouse or tunnel as it produces too much foliage in proportion to marrows.

HOW TO GROW

Seeds are big enough to be handled and sown in individual pots.

Seeds

Earliest time to sow: *indoors* end of February; *outdoors* mid-April.

Latest time to sow: *indoors* and *outdoors* mid-June.

Best time to sow: May.

Depth of sowing: 2cm (1in).

Germination time: 7 days.

Lifespan of seeds: 5 years.

Successional sowings: one single sowing, but 1–2 transplantings – plant out those ready first.

Plants

Earliest time to plant: early May.

Latest time to plant: end of June.

Best time to plant: May.

Stage of growth: when plants are about 18–20cm (7–8in) high.

Best aspect: sheltered, southerly aspect, on a gentle slope.

Best soil: a deep, rich, medium loam.

Soil preparation: dig a large hole, about 30cm (12in) deep and wide, add in manure or compost, mix with soil.

Space between plants: 2 metres (6.5ft).

Depth of planting: to soil mark on stem.

Growing situations: raised beds, open ground, but not in polytunnel.

Best varieties: Long Green Trailing, Long White Trailing, Greenbush.

Expected yield per plant: 2 to 4 marrows.

MANAGEMENT

* Harden-off plants before planting out.
* Keep free of weeds.
* Water in dry weather.

- Give liquid feeds as marrows are swelling.
- If too many marrows are formed, it is always better to reduce numbers by pulling off the smaller ones as they form. Those removed may be used as courgettes.

PESTS AND DISEASES

Pests: *Slugs* are the main problem from the time they are seedlings until maturity – the young plants will be severed at ground level; put out traps during wet weather.

Diseases: *Botrytis* is caused by cold, damp weather and excess manure; give plenty of ventilation and balanced fertiliser, reduce the level of nitrogen in the plant feed and increase the level of potassium – use organic tomato liquid feed, nettle or seaweed feed.

HARVESTING

Time from sowing to harvest: about 6 months.

When to harvest: when the fruit is about 45–50cm (18–20in) long and has stopped growing, usually September to mid-October.

Disposal of plant: when the first frosts burn off the leaves, pick the remaining fruits, pull the plant up and put it on the compost heap.

Storing: can be stored over winter in a dry, cool place, where they will last for a few months.

Good points: Easy for the beginner if grown from raised plants rather than from seed; follow transplant guidelines above. Will cope easily with weeds as marrows are rampant growers.

Bad points: Frost-tender when young. Does not like cold, wet weather.

DO

- Raise the plants in gentle heat in glasshouse or tunnel.
- Sow seed 2–3cm (1in) deep.
- Harden-off.
- Plant in rich soil.
- Do raise individual plants from a seed sown in compost in 7–8cm (3in) pots.
- Give plenty of space – as much as 3sq metres (3sq yards), 150cm x 150cm (5ft x 5ft).
- Prepare the ground well by deep digging 25–30cm (10–12in).
- Choose a sunny situation.
- Do provide protection against slugs.

DON'T

- Sow seeds too close together, minimum 5cm (2in).
- Plant out until danger of frost is over.
- Leave short of water in warm weather.
- Sow seeds too close together.
- Grow in glasshouse or tunnel as it will grow too rampant.

***TOP TIP

In cold, wet weather when there is little bee activity and no pollination, pick off the male flower and push it into the female flower (the one with the miniature marrow on it). Leave it there and pollination will take place. Remember, no pollination, no marrow.

WHITE TURNIPS

*EASY

Very closely related to turnips and swedes, but more delicate in flavour and earlier to mature. Being a brassica, it should not be sown in ground where cabbages or turnips were grown in the previous three to four years. Sow seeds where the plant will develop.

HOW TO GROW

Sow seeds thinly outdoors and thin-out to single plants.

Seeds

Earliest time to sow: end of March.

Latest time to sow: end July.

Best time to sow: end of April.

Best aspect: south.

Best soil: a well-drained, rich, medium loam.

Soil preparation: dig to eliminate perennial weeds and incorporate compost or dung.

Depth of sowing: 1cm (½in).

Space between seeds: sow thinly to approx 1cm (1/2in) apart.

Distance between rows: 45cm (18in).

Germination time: 8–10 days.

Lifespan of seeds: 5 years.

Thinning-out: thin-out to single plants spaced 10–15cm (4–6in) apart at 2–3 rough-leaf stage.

Growing situations: on the flat, drills, raised beds; indoors (early crops only) or outdoors.

Successional sowings: every 3–4 weeks.

Best varieties: Early Snowball, Greentop, Purpletop.

MANAGEMENT

- Keep weeds under control by hoe and by hand.
- Monitor constantly for slug attacks, especially in damp weather.
- Water in dry weather.
- Thin-out.
- Make successional sowings until early July.

PESTS AND DISEASES

See Swedes p163.

HARVESTING

Time from sowing to harvest: 6–12 weeks.

When to harvest: when turnips are about 5–6cm (2–3in) in diameter.

Storing: leave in ground.

Good points: Fast grower. Quick to germinate. One of the earliest crops to mature.

Bad points: Goes tough very quickly. Short season, so needs several sowings. Susceptible to Boron deficiency.

DO

- Observe rotation rules for brassicas.
- Sow in rich soil.
- Thin-out in time.

DON'T

- Sow too thickly
- Neglect weed control.
- Delay thinning-out.

HERBS

HERBS

*EASY

General note: all herbs are easy to grow, but they do need to be cared for like any other plant. Growing from seed isn't always easy, and, apart from parsley, it may be best to buy-in young plants. I have included instructions on growing from seed, however, for those who decide to do it that way.

Storing: it is possible to freeze some herbs for later use, but it's best to use them fresh, straight from the plant, and to strive for as long a growth span as possible.

BASIL

Basil is a half-hardy annual, meaning it is not fully hardy outside in our weather and is very challenged by cold, damp weather. It can be grown outdoors during June, July and August, but it needs protection of a glasshouse or polytunnel for the remainder of the year and will sometimes not survive a cold spell, even inside.

HOW TO GROW

Seeds

Germinate the seeds indoors at 12°C (65°F) in seed compost in a seed tray. Prick-out into cellular trays or individual pots as soon as it can be handled, taking 2–3 plants in a cluster. Harden-off before planting out

Earliest time to sow: end of March, early April.

Latest time to sow: mid-June.

Best time to sow: May.

Depth of sowing: 1cm (½ ins.)

Germination time: 12–14 days.

Lifespan of seeds: 2 years.

Successional sowings: sow every 3–4 weeks.

Plants

Will grow outdoors, but only in warm weather and after they have been hardened-off.

Earliest time to plant: early May.

Latest time to plant: mid-June.

Best time to plant: May.

Best aspect: sunny, southerly, sheltered position.

Best soil: a well-drained, rich, light to medium loam.

Soil preparation: dig deep, remove perennial weeds and incorporate manure and compost.

Space between plants: 25–30cm (10–12in).

Depth of planting: at soil mark on stem – can be more shallow but not deeper.

Growing situations: on the flat, drills, raised beds, containers (indoors or outdoors).

Best varieties: whatever is available.

MANAGEMENT

- Water regularly.
- Keep free of weeds.
- Harden-off before planting-out.

PESTS AND DISEASES

Pests: *Slugs* attack at all stages of plants life; slug traps are essential from seedling stage onwards. *Aphids* will attack under warm weather conditions and should be sprayed with washing-up liquid and water solution.

Diseases: *Botrytis* will attack and destroy the plants in cool, damp conditions. The best solution is to reduce humidity and raise temperature.

Good points: Grows fast. Can be grown in containers.
Bad points: Not fully hardy. Subject to many pests and diseases.

DO

• Sow in heat.
• Sow thinly.
• Harden-off.
• Protect from slugs.
• Make successional sowings.

DON'T

• Neglect weed control.
• Leave un-watered.
• Ignore slugs.

BAY LEAF

Bay leaf can vary in size from being a nice, miniature tree in a container to a big tree in the garden. It is evergreen, very hardy, ornamental and not known to succumb to any pests or diseases. It's botanical name is *Laurus nobilis*.

HOW TO GROW

It is best to buy-in or acquire a young plant.

Best time to plant: October–March.

Stage of growth: the shrub should be 35–45cm (14–18in).

Best aspect: south or south-west; will withstand wind.

Best soil: deep, well-drained, rich, medium to light loam.

Soil preparation: dig out all perennial weeds, add some compost and mix in well.

How to plant: dig a hole big enough to take the size of the root ball and plant firmly when soil and weather conditions are good – not raining, not frosty.

Growing situations: container, in the ground, raised beds.

Lifespan: 60–70 years.

MANAGEMENT

Trim to any desired shape in March/April.

PESTS AND DISEASES

None.

HARVESTING

How to harvest: remove single leaves rather than shoots, and select the older, more mature leaves.

Good points: Very hardy. Subject to few diseases and pests. Can be used as a shrub in shrub border. Survives well in a drought.

Bad points: Can grow out of control if left untrimmed. Has competitive roots.

DO

- Grow in a container if space is limited.
- Plant firmly.
- Grow in medium fertile soil.
- Train to shape and height.

DON'T

- Harvest for the first year.
- Allow it to go untrimmed.
- Plant near other trees or shrubs.

CHIVES

The chive plant is a member of the onion family, a perennial that goes dormant and dies back in winter, and each spring sends up fresh foliage. It is hardy in habit and easy to grow. It can be grown from seeds, but it is easier to buy-in ready-grown plants from a garden centre.

HOW TO GROW

Sow seeds indoors and plant out. Sow in trays with cells or in individual pots – a few seeds in each.

Seeds

Earliest time to sow: end of March to early April.

Latest time to sow: mid-June.

Best time to sow: May.

Depth of sowing: 1cm (½–¾in). Sow 3–4 seeds in each cell or pot.

Germination time: 14–21 days.

Lifespan of seeds: 2–3 years.

Successional sowings: one sowing usually sufficient.

Plants

Earliest time to plant: mid-April, from home-grown or bought-in plants.

Latest time to plant: mid-June.

Best time to plant: May.

Stage of growth: at 2–3 rough-leaf stage, after hardening-off.

Best aspect: southerly.

Best soil: fertile, well-drained, medium to light loam.

Soil preparation: dig deep, remove perennial weeds, add manure or compost.

Space between plants: 24–30cm (10–12in).

Distance between rows: 30–45cm (12–18in).

Depth of planting: plant to the same depth as the soil mark at the neck of the plant so that only about 1cm (½ in) of plant is visible above ground.

Growing situations: drills, on the flat, raised beds, containers or pots, in the open or under protection.

Lifespan: indefinite, if cared for properly. Lift up and divide every 5–6 years.

MANAGEMENT

- Keep weeds under control by regular hoeing; or grow in a black plastic mulch.

- Remove the flowers – they can be eaten – this helps the chives to stay green longer.

- Dig up and divide every 5–6 years – best to do this in spring as the new shoots are coming.

PESTS AND DISEASES

Relatively free, though it can pick up *white rot*; rotation is the only solution.

HARVESTING

Time from sowig to harvest: 12–14 months when growing from seed; grown from plants, 2–3 months.

When to harvest: harvest from April to early October outdoors.

Good points: Reliable in a wide range of soils. Attacked by very few pests and diseases.

Bad points: Dies down over winter. Needs to be divided every 5–6 years. Easily overcome by weeds if neglected.

DO

- Grow in good, fertile soil.
- Lift, subdivide and replant in fresh ground every 5–6 years.
- Keep weeds under control, especially perennial weeds.

DON'T

- Plant in badly drained or poor soil.
- Plant too deep or too shallow.
- Over-harvest the first year of planting.
- Plant where onions grew previously.

***TOP TIPS

- Divide up a home-grown plant or a plant from garden centre. Divide by pulling apart into smaller clusters – each one will grow if the roots are intact.

- If you grow them in a container, they can live indoors in winter and outdoors in summer, and give a much earlier crop.

CORIANDER

Coriander, or to give it its botanical name, *Coriandrum sativum*, is a member of the Umbelliferae (carrot) family. It can be difficult to grow because of a tendency to bolt.

HOW TO GROW

Seeds

Can be sown in seed trays, pots or cellular trays, but the real risk is allowing the seedlings to dry out before hardening-off and transplanting takes place.

Earliest time to sow: early April.

Latest time to sow: mid-June.

Best time to sow: May.

Depth of sowing: 1cm (½in).

Germination time: 10–14 days.

Lifespan of seeds: 3 years.

Successional sowings: every 4 weeks

Plants

Earliest time to plant: early May after hardening-off.

Latest time to plant: mid-June.

Best time to plant: May.

Stage of growth: 2–3 rough-leaf stage.

Best aspect: a warm, sunny, southerly aspect.

Best soil: well-drained, deep, rich, light to medium loam.

Soil preparation: dig out perennial weeds and dig in compost, especially in soils where fertility is low.

Space between plants: 25–30cm (10–12in).

Distance between rows: 30–35cm (12–14in).

Depth of planting: to soil mark on stem.

Growing situations: drills, beds, raised beds, containers; most likely to succeed in glasshouse or polytunnel.

MANAGEMENT

- Bolting is the real problem with coriander. Any setback, such as sudden very high or low temperature, shortage of water or nutrients or delayed transplanting will cause bolting. Never allow the temperature to rise or fall suddenly.

- Keep in a state of continuous growth by keeping up a regular water and food supply.

- Weeds are a real threat, so keep them under control.

PESTS AND DISEASES

Pests: *Slugs*; put down slug traps early and regularly.

HARVESTING

Time from sowing to harvesting: 3 months.

How to harvest: cut, don't pull.

Good points: It is an annual. Grows fast from seed. Easily propagated. Pests and disease do not bother it.

Bad point: It can be over-run with weeds.

DO

- Plant in good, well-ventilated area.
- Sow seed inside.
- Harden-off and plant-out.
- Keep free of weeds.

DON'T

- Plant in the shade.
- Allow weeds get out of control.

MARJORAM

A member of the Origanum family, *Origanum majorana*. It's a herbaceous perennial herb that is frost-hardy, and available in a number of different varieties. It can be grown from seed, though this is quite difficult and I wouldn't recommend it as it is not worth the trouble. You'll get better results from planting cuttings taken in summer, or by dividing the plants in spring. You can source plants at a good garden centre or from a friend who is growing it already.

HOW TO GROW

Plant cuttings in pots and harden-off, or buy-in small plants.

Plants

Earliest time to plant: mid-April.

Latest time to plant: mid-June.

Best time to plant: May.

Stage of growth: when plants have developed a good head, are growing well and are hardened-off.

Best aspect: a southerly, sheltered situation.

Best soil: well-drained, rich, medium loam.

Soil preparation: dig deep, remove perennial weeds, incorporate well-rotted manure and compost.

Space between plants: 30cm (12in).

Distance between rows: 30-35cm (12–14in).

Growing situations: raised beds, containers, drills or on the flat; indoors or outdoors.

MANAGEMENT

- Control of weeds is essential right from the start and throughout the life of the plant. Use a black woven plastic mulch or carry out frequent hand-weeding or hoeing.

- To propagate: divide the plants in spring, or take cuttings 10–15cm (4–6in) long and pot-up in compost until they root.

PESTS AND DISEASES

Apart from *slugs*, there is no serious pest or disease that attacks marjoram; apply slug traps throughout growing time.

HARVESTING

Time from planting to harvest: about 6 months.

Good points: A hardy perennial. Grows in a wide range of soils. Easily propagated by root cuttings in spring.

Bad points: Dislikes heavy, clay soils. Will not tolerate poor drainage.

DO

- Plant in well-drained soil.

- Plant in a sunny site.
- Divide up occasionally, every 3–4 years or so.

DON'T

- Allow weeds to grow over it.
- Don't plant in poorly drained soil.

MINT

There are many forms of mint in cultivation. Most are perennials, with a vigorous underground spreading root system. Annual mints are also grown. Mints vary in height and growth habit, and in flowers and strength. The most common are peppermint, spearmint and field mint. They are all perennials and grow very easily from cuttings (portion of the root) taken in spring. They all require the same conditions and methods.

HOW TO GROW

Grown from cuttings or small plants from a garden centre or from other gardeners.

Plants

Earliest time to plant: early April.

Latest time to plant: mid-May.

Best time to plant: May.

Best aspect: virtually any aspect, but must be well-drained.

Best soil: any free-draining, medium to heavy loam.

Soil preparation: dig out perennial weeds, break up lumps.

Space between plants: 30–35cm (12–14in); plant in groups or clusters.

Growing situations: open ground, raised beds, containers or large pots; outdoors or indoors in pots.

MANAGEMENT

- Remove flowering heads as they appear.
- Cut the whole plant back to ground level each autumn.
- Dig up and divide the roots every 4–5 years.

PESTS AND DISEASES

None.

HARVESTING

Time from planting to harvest: 6–8 weeks.

Cropping time: April to October.

Good points: Very vigorous. Very hardy. Very pest and disease resistant.

Bad points: Very aggressive grower.

DO

- Grow in a confined area.
- Grow in well-drained soil.
- Grow in a sunny aspect.
- Lift and divide every few years.

DON'T

- Plant near other herbs.
- Over-feed.
- Allow weeds to grow into it.

***TOP TIP

Confine the roots with physical barriers of metal, stone or plastic to prevent it invading the garden.

PARSLEY

The most popular of all herbs in Ireland. It is a biennial – it grows the first year and over-winters; the following spring it produces a long, flowering stem and a seed head, and dies. The scarcest time for parsley is at the end of June after the old crop has gone to seed and the young plants still have not grown to sufficient size.

Types: curled-leaf type and flat-leaf type; flat-leaf has a stronger flavour.

Number of plants needed for average use: 6–10 good plants.

HOW TO GROW

Seeds

Earliest time to sow: *indoors* end of February–mid-March for transplanting; *outdoors* mid-April.

Latest time to sow without transplanting: *outdoors* mid-July. If planted in a seedbed, thin-out, do not transplant.

Best time to sow: May.

Depth of sowing: 1cm (½ in).

Germination time: 18–21 days.

Lifespan of seeds: 4–5 years if stored well.

Seed-sowing: sow 4–5 seeds per cell.

Successional sowings: two sowings normally, one in spring and one in summer.

Plants

Earliest time to plant: early April, after hardening-off.

Latest time to plant: end of July.

Best time to plant: June.

Best aspect: southerly.

Best soil: deep, medium rich loam, well drained.

Soil preparation: dig deep, eliminate any perennial weeds. Break any soil lumps and remove clods.

Space between plants: 15cm (6in).

Distance between rows: 30cm (12in).

Depth of planting: to soil mark on stem.

Growing situations: drills, on the flat, raised beds, containers or pots; indoors or outdoors.

Rotation: parsley belongs to the same family as parsnips, carrots and celery, so parsley should not be sown until there has been a gap of 3–4 years in these crops.

Best varieties: Moss Curled; many other varieties available in curly and flat-leaved and all are quite successful.

MANAGEMENT

* Weeds will smother the crop if left uncontrolled.
* *Feed*: give base dressing to soil, but don't add further top dressing.
* Flowering stem emerges when cropping period is over, pull up plant and place in compost heap.

PESTS AND DISEASES

Slugs will attack emerging parsley seedlings; put out trap.

HARVESTING

Time from sowing to harvest: 4–5 months.

Time from planting plants to harvest: you can begin to

harvest when it has 4–5 leaves, about 3–4 weeks.

Good Points: Virtually trouble free, few pests and diseases. Will grow in a wide range of soils. Winter hardy. Can be used all year round.

Bad points: None.

DO

- Plant it or sow in deep, well-drained, rich soil.
- Sow it on time to allow it to develop during the summer.
- Sow seeds thinly.
- Sow or plant in weed-free ground.
- Thin-out to 15cm (6in) apart if sown too thickly.
- Sow or plant in a container or pot if short of garden space.
- Plant out between April and June.
- Make two sowings in the year – spring and summer.

DON'T

- Sow or plant after carrots, parsnips, celery, or a previous crop of parsley.
- Don't sow seeds more than 1cm (½in) deep.
- Over-feed with manures or give liquid feed.
- Plant in ground if perennial weeds are present.

***TOP TIP

Buy-in pot of plants in spring and divide up before planting out.

ROSEMARY

Rosemary is a shrub and is equally at home in the shrub border as in the herb garden. A number of varieties exist, varying in their growth habit and height.

HOW TO GROW

Rosemary is propagated by cuttings, 10–15cm (4–6in) long, taken from the parent bush in spring.

Plants

Earliest time to plant: if planting in the ground, it is normally planted between November and early April; plant in a container at any time of year.

Best aspect: southerly.

Best soil: deep, well-drained, rich, light to medium loam.

Soil preparation: dig out perennial weeds, add in manure and compost in a hole big enough to take the root of the shrub. Plant as deep as the soil mark on stem and firm the soil around the root.

Growing situations: shrub border, herb garden, raised beds; in containers for a limited number of years before it gets potbound; outdoors.

Lifespan of shrub: 10–15 years.

Best varieties: several varieties, usually bought for ornamental value – the flavour is usually the same.

MANAGEMENT

- Shorten back the shoots produced in the spring to encourage branching and bushiness.

PESTS AND DISEASES

None.

HARVESTING

Time from planting to first cuttings: small amounts may be cut off a few weeks after planting in spring. Do not take leaves from shrubs planted in the winter.

Good points: Hardy shrub. Has a very long life.
Bad points: Can be slow to get established. Likes warm situations.

DO

- Plant it as a small shrub.
- Plant in a well-drained soil.
- Plant into weed-free ground.

DON'T

- Plant in poor, badly drained ground.
- Plant in a cold, exposed situation.
- Cut into old wood when using leaves.

SAGE

Sage is a small, soft-wooded shrub, but generally has a short life, 4–5 years. If grown from seed, it can be harvested in the second year, but if grown from a bought-in plant in the early summer, it can be harvested within a matter of weeks, even before planting it out. It is usually grown from bought-in plants.

HOW TO GROW

Seeds

Sow seed singly in pots or cellular trays.

Earliest time to sow: *inside* end of March for transplanting outside after hardening-off; *outside* mid-June for thinning-out.

Latest time to sow: early June.

Best time to sow: May.

Depth of sowing: 1cm (½in).

Germination time: 14–21 days depending on temperature.

Lifespan of seeds: 2–3 years.

Successional sowings: one sowing is usually sufficient to raise 4–5 plants.

Plants

Earliest time to plant: plants raised indoors in March–April should be planted out in mid-to late May, after hardening-off.

Latest time to plant: mid-June.

Best time to plant: late May to mid-June.

Stage of growth: plant should have 3–4 rough leaves and be 12–15cm (5–6in) high.

Best aspect: southerly, not shaded.

Best soil: deep, well-drained, rich medium loam.

Soil preparation: dig deep 25–30cm (10–12in); remove all perennial weeds and add in manure or compost. Make hole big enough to take root ball and plant firmly.

Space between plants: 45cm (18in).

Growing situations: open garden, raised beds or containers; outdoors.

Best varieties: *Salvia officionalis* or Common Sage is the variety most often planted, but many other species are available.

MANAGEMENT
• Keep free of weeds.

PESTS AND DISEASES
None.

HARVESTING
Time from sowing to harvest: 12–14 months.
Time from bought-in plants to harvest: 3–4 months.
Lifespan of plants: 4–5 years; can last longer but will not be as productive.

Good points: Small enough to be grown in a container. Ornamental and decorative. Can be grown from seed.
Bad points: Short-lived. Gets ragged and leggy with age.

DO
• Plant in a warm, sunny situation.
• Plant in a dry, well-drained soil.

DON'T
• Plant in the shade.
• Plant in a wet situation.
• Over-harvest in the first year.

***TOP TIP

Grow a number of different varieties to enjoy the variations in flavour.

THYME

Thyme is a lovely herb to grow – it is edible, ornamental and scented. It grows in the form of a miniature shrublet. It can be grown from seed, but is difficult to raise. It is a very popular herb and is usually bought-in as a young plant and put in the herb garden.

HOW TO GROW

Seed is sown indoors, and plants transplanted outdoors. Plants are available at garden centres usually from mid-April onwards, and are suitable for transplanting, but best grown on for a few weeks to harden-off.

Seeds

Earliest time to sow: indoors with heat, end of March to early April.

Latest time to sow: mid-June.

Best time to plant: May.

Depth of sowing: seed is not covered, scatter on to compost and press in.

Best compost for sowing: sandy loam.

Optimum germination temperature: 13°C (65°F) – temperature is important; if it's cold, sow much later, around early June.

Germination time: 14–21 days.

Lifespan of seeds: 3–5 years.

Successional sowings: one sowing should suffice to raise enough plants.

Plants

Earliest time to plant: mid-May after hardening off.

Latest time to plant: mid-July.

Best time to plant: throughout the summer, stage of growth is best guideline.

Stage of growth: plant out when plants are 3–5cm (1–2in) tall after hardening-off.

Best aspect: southerly.

Best soil: light, sandy loam, well drained.

Soil preparation: dig deep, remove perennial weeds and large stones, make a nice, friable seedbed, as plants are small. There is no need to add manure or compost.

Space between plants: 20–25cm (8–10in).

Distance between rows: 45cm (18in).

Depth of planting: not deeper than soil mark on stem.

Growing situations: beds, drills, on the flat, containers or pots; indoors or outdoors.

Lifespan: up to 10 years.

Best varieties: most varieties perform well.

MANAGEMENT

- Trim off blossoms as they appear, but avoid removing leaves if possible.
- To prevent weeds, plant into a black plastic mulch.

PESTS AND DISEASES

Pests: Usually *slugs* at the seedling stage – put out traps.

Diseases: Relatively disease free.

HARVESTING

Time from sowing to harvest: 7–8 months.

Time from planting to harvest: 3 months.

How to harvest: cut off, rather than pulling off, the tips of the shoots as required, taking care not to cut back into the harder wood, which will not shoot again if cut.

Good points: A long-lasting plant. Will grow in poor soils. Can be grown in a raised bed or container.

Bad points: Will not tolerate poor drainage. Dislikes cold, exposed situations. Easily killed off by over-cutting.

DO

- Choose a very free-draining soil.
- Plant in a warm, sunny situation.
- Grow from a young plant.

DON'T

- Try to raise from seed until you have a bit of experience.
- Plant in a wet soil.
- Plant in the shade.
- Over-harvest in the early years.
- Allow weeds to overgrow the plant.

SOFT FRUITS

SOFT FRUITS

This is the collective name for strawberries, raspberries, gooseberries, loganberries, blackcurrants, red currants, blueberries and a few more lesser-known hybrid berries. They should occupy a permanent part in the garden, preferably grouped together to make it easier to net them.

***TOP TIP

If a lot of soft fruits are to be grown, then it is better to make a permanent walk-in frame or cage, covered by mesh wire or plastic netting to protect them from birds. Buy the net first and then measure out the bed to suit the net. Always have the net about 30cm (12in) above the plants.

BLACKCURRANTS

*EASY

Formerly a very popular crop in Ireland and renowned for its Vitamin C content. Becoming popular again, with newer varieties that are bigger and easier to grow. Very attractive to birds and a net is needed to prevent the fruit being taken. One bush should yield around 10 kilos (22lb) of fruit.

***TOP TIP

Blackcurrants produce most of their fruit on young wood. The aim should be to encourage as much young growth as possible by judicious pruning and manuring, aiming to cut out as much as possible of the old wood.

HOW TO GROW

Plants

Best time to plant: from October to early April.

Best aspect: south, well sheltered.

Best soil: deep, well-drained, rich, medium loam.

Soil preparation: dig deep and root out any perennial weeds. Dig a hole 30cm (1ft) wide and 45cm (18in) deep where individual bushes are to be planted, and add in manure and compost and mix with soil.

Minimum spacing between bushes: 180cm (6ft) apart each way.

How to plant: put the roots of the bush into the hole, down deeper than the soil mark and press the soil back in around the roots. Plant firmly.

Growing situations: on the flat, drills, raised beds or containers. Avoid frost hollows as blackcurrants are subject to damage at blossom time. Outdoors.

Lifespan: on average 10–12 years or longer.

Best varieties: Ben Lomond, Ben Alder, Wellington XXX.

MANAGEMENT

- Weed control is an all-year-round job; alternatively, you could plant bushes into ground covered with black plastic ground mulch.
- **First pruning**: immediately after planting; cut back to within 7–10cm (3–4in) of soil level to encourage young growth from soil level.

- **Annual pruning**: done between November and March, and entails cutting back one third in number of the oldest branches (darker coloured) back down to ground level.
- Give an annual liberal dressing of manure or compost around the base of the bush without digging in.

PESTS AND DISEASES

Pests: *Birds* are a problem and netting is the only solution. *Aphids* can be serious in warm, dry weather and plant should be sprayed with washing-up liquid or soft soap and water solution as soon as the first aphids are seen.

Diseases: The main disease is *Botrytis*, usually present in cold, damp weather. The bushes can be affected by various viral and fungal diseases and it is important to get bushes from a reliable source.

HARVESTING

Time from planting and first crop: 15–18 months.

Propagation: easy from short cuttings, 20–24cm (8–10in), taken in October /November and pushed into the ground to about half their length.

DO

- Plant in a frost-free, sheltered site.
- Choose a deep, rich, medium loam.
- Plant in a free-draining soil.
- Plant at least 1.8 metres (6ft) apart each way.
- Get bushes from a reliable source.
- Dig in well-rotted dung or compost before planting.
- Prune back hard after planting.

- Plant a reliable and suitable variety.

DON'T

- Plant in an exposed site.
- Plant in a frost hollow.
- Plant bushes of doubtful quality.
- Plant in poor soil.
- Plant in weed-infested ground.
- Plant near other bushes or trees.

BLUEBERRIES
*MEDIUM–DIFFICULT

The blueberry is a close relative of the wild whortleberry or bilberry. It likes an acid soil that is rich and free-draining. The bush is small, and needs to be managed well, with regular pruning and feeding. Early crops can be grown inside in containers. Source: most garden centres stock them, but they can also be ordered from plant sources.

HOW TO GROW

Plants

Best time to plant: March is best, but can be planted from November to early March.

Best aspect: southerly, with good shelter.

Best soil: free-draining, rich, light to medium loam, with a low pH (below 5.5), very acidic.

Soil preparation: dig deep and root out any perennial weeds.

Minimum spacing between bushes: allow 1.5 metres x 1.5 metres (5ft x 5ft).

How to plant: dig a hole 30cm (1ft) wide and 45cm (18in) deep where individual bushes are to be planted, and add in manure and compost and mix with soil. Put the roots of the bush into the hole down deeper than the soil mark and press the soil back in around the roots.

Growing situations: drills, on the flat, raised beds or containers. Outdoors.

Shelter: it is essential to provide good shelter as this aids pollination.

Drainage: though often associated with boggy, peaty soils, the blueberry requires very good drainage, while at the same time it will not tolerate a shortage of water in dry weather.

Mulch: a mulch 10–12cm (4–5in) thick of tree bark or pine/spruce leaves is advisable.

Lifespan: 15–20 years.

Best varieties: use whatever is available.

Expected yield per bush: 3kg (6.5lb) per mature bush (3–4 years old).

MANAGEMENT

- Weed control is vital as they compete for nutrients and water, and pulling up established weeds can damage the shallow roots and lead to crop reduction. Constant weeding is needed, or use black woven plastic sheeting as part of a weed-control programme.
- Feeding with a high nitrogen content plant food during the growing season is essential.

- Pruning is done sparingly by removing a few older shoots every 3–4 years, November–March. The fruits are borne on the older shoots.

PESTS AND DISEASES

Pests: *Birds* are the chief problem, and nets are the only solution.

HARVESTING

Time from planting to harvest: depends on maturity of bush planted; can take 3–4 years.

When to harvest: the berries are fit to harvest when they are well coloured and feel slightly soft.

Good points: Will grow in acid soils. Subject to few pests and diseases.

Bad points: Can take a long time to crop. Blossom subject to frost damage.

DO

- Plant in acidic soil
- Plant in a well-drained, rich soil

DON'T

- Add compost with lime or high pH.
- Allow weeds out of control.
- Allow plants to run short of water.

GOOSEBERRIES

*EASY

Gooseberries are making a comeback in popularity after being almost totally neglected in the past twenty to thirty years. They are extremely hardy and reliable, easy to grow and rich in minerals and vitamins.

HOW TO GROW

Plants

Best time to plant: October–March.

Best aspect: will tolerate any aspect, including a northerly one, but best and earliest crops are got from bushes grown in a southerly aspect. Shelter promotes good pollination for early crops.

Best soil: deep, rich, medium loam, well drained.

Soil preparation: dig deep and root out any perennial weeds.

Minimum spacing between bushes: 180cm (6ft) apart each way.

Space required per bush: 3–3.5sq metres (35–36sq ft).

Shape of bush at planting: 2–3 shoots, with a clear stem of 30cm (12in).

How to plant: dig a hole 30cm (1ft) wide and 45cm (1.5ft) deep where individual bushes are to be planted, and add in manure and compost and mix with soil. Put the roots of the bush into the hole down deeper than the soil mark and press the soil back in around the roots.

Growing situations: on the flat, drills, containers, raised beds or trained against a wall. Outdoors.

Expected yield per bush: 3–4 kg (6.5–9lb).

Lifespan: 20 years, and longer if well managed.

Best varieties: there are three types: green, red and yellow; Early Sulphur (yellow), Invicta (green), Whinham's Industry (red), Careless (green), Leveller (green), White Lion (green), May Duke (red).

MANAGEMENT

- **Pruning**: this is an essential annual exercise, carried out between November and March. Cut out dead and diseased wood. Cut out branches crossing one another. Cut out branches too near the ground. Keep centre of bush clear to make picking easier and shape to an open shape. Shorten shoots over 30cm (12in) back to half their length; remove tips from all other shoots – about 2cm (1in).

- Add manure or compost to the ground around the roots after the leaves have dropped off each autumn. Do not dig in or disturb the roots.

- Weed control: use woven black plastic mulch.

PESTS AND DISEASES

Pests: *Aphids* infest the growing tips and can damage fruit development; spray with a solution of water and washing-up liquid or soft soap. *Gooseberry sawfly* can skeletonise the leaves and cause serious crop loss; spray with a solution of salt – a tablespoonful dissolved in 4–5 litres (1 gallon) water.

Another very effective way is to place a newspaper or sheet of plastic under the bush and shake the bush vigorously. Leave the birds pick away at the worms. Repeat if necessary the following week. *Birds,* especially *tits*: these birds pick the buds off the bushes in the winter in search of grubs or maggots (they don't like the fruits), and after a bad attack no fruit will grow. Nets over the individual bushes in the autumn and left on until bud break (April) will prevent this happening.

Diseases: *American gooseberry mildew* – this is readily identified by the brown, felt-like covering or mould on developing fruit, which starts off as a white, powdery covering. Control and prevent this by removing tips of shoots (about 2–3cm (1–2in) in winter.

HARVESTING

Time from planting to harvest: 15–18 months.

Normal harvest time: mid-June to mid-July.

Yield of fruit: 6–8kg, (14–20lbs) of fruit after 5–6 years.

Propagation: cuttings should be 25–30cm (10–12in) long, taken from good, healthy cropping bushes, with all except the top 3–4 buds removed, from October to December/January. Place 10 or 12 of them in a bucket or container of sand or sandy soil, and by March/April some roots should have developed. Success rate is around 10%. Plant out, about 30cm (12in) apart, for one year before planting into final quarters the following winter.

Good points: Very tolerant of soil types. Very reliable croppers. Fruit can be frozen and stored. Very rich source of vitamins and minerals. Bushes have a long life. Fruit not attractive to birds.

Bad points: Difficult to pick fruits. Difficult to prune. Very hard to get rid of weeds that infest the base of the bush.

DO

- Give it plenty room.
- Grow it in a sheltered situation.
- Make sure the soil is well drained.
- Get rid of all perennial weeds before planting.
- Plant between October and end of March.
- Purchase a plant with a clear leg or stem for easy training.
- Give a balanced feed high in potassium, such as wood ash or seaweed feed.
- Give at least 3–4sq metres (35–36sq ft) per bush of ground space.

DON'T

- Plant in a cold, wet or poor soil.
- Plant near other trees or shrubs or bushes.
- Allow weeds go out of control.
- Plant in badly drained soils.

***TOP TIPS

- Grow gooseberry bushes with a single leg rather than many stems, as it is easier to shape and manage.
- Gooseberries fruit on new *and* old wood and so are suitable for training as fans or espaliers against a wall or trellis.

LOGANBERRIES

*EASY

A good, reliable fruit, with a very distinctive, tart taste. Can be grown against a wall or fence, but requires plenty of space as the canes can grow as long as 360cm (12ft). Birds will attack them, but are not as attracted to them as to raspberries.

HOW TO GROW

Plants

Best aspect: any aspect except north – and some shelter is needed.

Best soil: deep, well-drained, rich, medium loam.

Growing situations: on the flat, container, or up against a wall. Not suitable for raised beds because of the long, trailing stems.

Soil preparation: dig deep and clear off any perennial weeds before adding manure and compost mixed with soil into a hole 30cm (12in) deep and 24cm (18in) in diameter. Put the plant into the hole, placing the soil and compost around the roots and firmly packing it. Horizontal wires are needed to support the long, trailing canes.

When to plant: October to March.

Space between plants: 3.5–4 metres (12–14ft) apart.

Planting depth: plant them deep enough to cover the roots without having stems below soil level.

Lifespan: 20 years.

Best varieties: Thornless, or LY95. May need to be ordered from a nursery.

MANAGEMENT

* **First pruning**: prune back the cane or canes to about 45cm to prevent fruiting in first year.
* **Annual pruning**: The old shoots are cut back to soil level after they have finished fruiting. The young shoots that are to fruit the following year are shortened back by about 30cm (12in) and then tied onto the wires or wall.
* Weeds should be controlled throughout the growing season.
* A dressing of manure or compost is given around the roots, but not dug in during the late autumn or winter.

PESTS AND DISEASES

Very good resistance.

HARVESTING

Time to first crop from planting: 15–18 months.

Good point: Reliable croppers.

Bad points: Produces long, spreading branches. New shoots produced every year. Very thorny. Requires a lot of space. Requires a structure to be trained onto.

DO

* Give plenty of space.
* Plant in a deep, rich soil.
* Plant in a warm situation.

DON'T

- Plant close together.
- Plant in poor soil.
- Plant in a cold situation.

Blackberries, tayberries, tummelberries, sunberries, wineberries, boysenberries are all grown in the same way, so these instructions offer a great variety of crops. These fruits all have their own individual taste, but all are grown, pruned and trained in a similar fashion.

RASPBERRIES
(summer fruiting)

*EASY

A wonderful, much-loved fruit, but a most unruly crop, as they creep gradually from the place they were planted originally. A woodland plant that thrives on soils high in humus or organic matter. The fruit is borne on canes, produced the previous year. Raspberry canes need to be secured to wires on stakes to prevent them being blown around by the wind. They are easy to grow and there are autumn croppers as well as summer varieties. Can be grown inside, in glasshouses or tunnels, but should be in containers and not planted into the ground. They can be got at many garden centres, or ordered from many plant sources.

HOW TO GROW

Plants

Best aspect: any aspect, very tolerant; well sheltered gentle slope is best.

Best soil: deep, fertile, medium loam, with a good supply of humus.

Soil preparation: clear off perennial weeds and dig in manure or compost.

Growing situations: on the flat, containers, raised beds (suitable for growing, but may be a bit high for picking fruit).

Time of planting: November to March.

Depth of planting: as deep as the soil mark on the stem, ensuring the bud at the base of the cane is just 2–3cm (1in) below soil level.

Distance between canes: 25–30cm (10–12in).

Space between rows: 1.8–2.4 metres (6–8ft) depending on height of variety (a tall variety, like Malling Jewel, needs 2.4 metres [8ft] between rows). Crops such as lettuce or strawberries can be grown between the rows for the first year or two.

Best varieties: Malling Jewel, Glen Clova, Malling Leo.

Number of canes needed per household: 20–25.

Yield of fruit per foot of row: 200–250 grams (½–¾lb).

MANAGEMENT

• *Weeds*: control weeds when bushes are small. Perennial weeds, especially, should be controlled as they will invade the root space of raspberries and seriously affect cane growth and cropping.

Pruning

- **First pruning**: immediately after planting, cut the canes back to a height of 45cm (18in). The purpose of this is to prevent fruiting in the first year, so as to divert energy into cane production and allow foliage develop from the lower buds.
- **Annual pruning**: October/November, when fruiting is finished. Cut canes that have fruited back to ground level. Thin-out weak shoots left, to 20–25cm (8–10in) apart.
- Secure young canes to wires in October.

PESTS AND DISEASES

Pests: *Birds* are the main pests and nets should be put over the canes. Get the net first and shape the planting to suit the measurements of the net.

Diseases: *Botrytis* affects the fruit at time of ripening and usually occurs in damp, wet conditions. Good ventilation helps to reduce or eliminate the disease. Other diseases of the canes and roots which lead to poor cropping are largely avoided by planting certified disease-free canes.

HARVESTING

Time from planting to first fruit: 15–18 months.

Propagation: raspberries are propagated by digging up the fresh canes (current year's growth) with a sharp spade in autumn as the leaves are dropping. Ensure there is a bud at the base of each cane and plant to a new position. Propagate only from canes that have a good cropping history.

Good points: Crop in the second year after planting. Long life, up to 10-12 years. Heavy croppers. Easy to maintain. Few pests and diseases.

Bad points: Tend to be invasive in garden. Need staking and support. Require wide spacing between rows. Weeds need to be controlled.

DO

- Choose a sunny, sheltered site.
- Plant in a deep, well-drained, fertile soil.
- Clear the site of perennial weeds before planting.
- Plant at the right depth.
- Give sufficient space between canes.
- Give plenty of dung or compost before planting.
- Get canes from a reliable source.
- Support canes with wire and stakes.

DON'T

- Plant in cold, exposed situations.
- Plant in poor, shallow soils.
- Plant into weedy ground.
- Plant too close together.
- Grow vegetables too near the roots.
- Plant in shade of trees.

(autumn-fruiting)

*EASY

Autumn-fruiting raspberries have become very popular, and are easy to grow and trouble free.

HOW TO GROW

Plant as for raspberries except for timing given here.

Plants

When to plant: late spring (April–May).

Best varieties: Autumn Bliss; Full's Gold is a yellow raspberry, with good flavour and good yields.

HARVESTING

Time from planting to harvesting: 6 months.

RED/WHITE CURRANTS

*EASY

Lovely jewel-like berries, easy to grow; sharp but pleasant to eat or to add to other summer fruits; they can be eaten uncooked or made into a jam or jelly. Birds love them and there is no point in growing red currants without netting them. White currants are a variety of red currants and are treated in the exact same way. More closely related to gooseberries than to blackcurrants.

HOW TO GROW

Plants

Best aspect: southerly.

Best soil type: light to medium-rich loam.

Growing situations: on the flat, drills, containers, raised beds, or trained against a wall.

Soil preparation: dig deep and root out any perennial weeds. Dig a hole 30cm (1ft) wide and 45cm (1.5ft) deep where individual bushes are to be planted and add in manure and compost and mix with soil. Put the roots of the bush into the hole, down deeper than the soil mark, and press the soil back in around the roots.

Best time to plant: November to April.

Space required per bush: 4sq metres (35–36sq ft) each.

Depth of planting: plant to the soil mark on the stem, not any deeper.

Age of bush at planting time: 2 years old.

Shape of bush: umbrella shaped, single stem with radiating branches at 30cm (12in) above soil level.

Lifespan: up to 20 years, with good management.

Best varieties: Laxton, Red Lake, Junifer.

MANAGEMENT

- **Pruning**: pruning consists of cutting back the young shoots each year after leaf fall by one third of their length. If growth is poor, shorten back each shoot to half its length.
- Put manure or compost on the ground, in winter, around the stems without digging it in.
- Keep weeds under control. Use woven black plastic mulch to suppress them or use the hoe regularly.

PESTS AND DISEASES

Pests: *Aphids* and *gooseberry sawfly* attack red currants and the same control measures apply as for gooseberries (see p217).

HARVESTING

Time from planting to first crop: 15–18 months.

Propagation: take cuttings from current year's growth, 30cm (12in) long, in October/November; push 15cm (6in) into the ground and there will be roots on them by the following March or April, when they should either be planted out to their permanent situation or put into a large pot or container and grown on for a year.

Good points: Easy to grow. Reliable croppers. Resistant to most pests and diseases.

Bad points: Nets needed to keep birds off fruit. Young shoots are brittle and break off easily.

DO

- Plant in a warm place.
- Provide shelter.
- Plant in medium-rich loam.

DON'T

- Plant in a cold site.
- Plant in poor soil.
- Grow without nets.
- Plant in shady situation.

STRAWBERRIES

*MEDIUM TO DIFFICULT

A fast-growing perennial fruit that will crop within the first year of planting and lasts 3–5 years. It is a woodland type of plant that is very adaptable to various soil and climatic conditions. It will repay any attention given with a good crop of fresh, flavoursome fruit. The plants fruit the first year, giving a small crop of large fruits; in the second year, a large crop of large fruits; and in the third year, a larger crop of smaller fruit.

HOW TO GROW

With strawberries, you plant 'runners' which are young plants that grew off the parent plant in the previous season. Strawberry runners can be purchased at fruit nurseries or garden centres.

Number of plants needed for a household: 50–60 plants, made up of one-third one-year-olds, one-third two-year-olds and one-third three-year-olds.

Plants

Best aspect: southerly, not too sheltered.

Best location: a well-sheltered, gentle slope, facing south.

Best soil: a weed-free, deep, medium, well-drained loam.

Space between plants: 45cm (18in).

Distance between rows: 60–75cm (2–2.5ft).

Soil preparation: dig well, break down all lumps, remove perennial weeds, add compost or manure.

Planting depth: the crown or bud of the plant should be at or just below ground level.

Growing situations: drills, flat ground, raised beds, containers and barrels, polytunnels, glasshouses; can be grown between rows of apple trees or blackcurrant and gooseberry bushes, but only for 1–2 years.

Planting season:

early indoor crops, September/October (or plant outdoors in containers if you are caught for space, and bring in in January/February).

outdoor crops: September/October or March/April.

Best varieties:

Cambridge Vigour – a very good early variety, good flavour.

Cambridge Favourite – good main-crop variety with fair resistance to diseases; high yields and good in poor weather conditions.

Royal Sovereign – a very old favourite, but hard to get a good strain of plants. Reputed to have the best flavour of all. Not the heaviest yielder and short-lived.

Elsanta – probably the favourite of the modern-day varieties, good disease resistance, heavy cropper and excellent flavour; large fruits, mid-season and suitable for indoor as well as outdoor use.

Symphony – a late variety, but reliable and a heavy cropper.

Judibell – a very late variety, but not a heavy cropper.

MANAGEMENT

- Keep free of weeds – by hoe and hand-weeding. An alternative is to plant the runners through small holes made in woven plastic mulch laid down on the ground after soil preparation. The holes, 2–3 cm (1–2in) diameter, are either cut or burned out, and made at the spacings for planting given above.
- Keep the birds and slugs off.
- Control unwanted runners (these are the small plants produced at the end of a shoot as the natural means of propagation) by cutting them off every autumn. The runners may be rooted directly into the ground or in a small flower pot for lifting later to a permanent position. Always select the biggest and strongest runners from the healthiest parent plants, and put the rest on the compost heap.
- Spread some manure or compost over the plants after tidying up the unwanted runners, but only if there is poor growth.
- *Watering*: if fruit is swelling during a dry spell, then give plenty of water; if grown in barrels or containers, lack of water will lead to partial or total loss, or small fruit.

PESTS AND DISEASES

Pests: *Birds* are a problem and netting is essential. *Aphids* can destroy a crop before the fruit ripens and should be sprayed with a solution of water and washing-up liquid or soft soap. *Slugs* can be controlled by slug traps put out from the time the fruit forms until it ripens.

Diseases: The most serious disease of the fruit is *Botrytis*, which is at its worst in cold, damp weather. Ventilation helps to prevent or control the disease. Other diseases (viral and fungal) which affect cropping indirectly are prevented by planting runners from certified plant propagators.

HARVESTING

Time from planting to crop production: 3 months from spring planting and 7–8 months from autumn planting.

Good points: Crops very soon after planting. Easily planted. Lifespan of plants, 4–5 years.

Bad points: Easily overcome by weeds. Must be netted against birds. Subject to many diseases and pests.

DO

- Plant in a sunny situation.
- Plant in a weed-free, soil-rich area.
- Plant in rich, well-drained soil.
- Add manure or compost, mix in well.
- Get plants from a reliable, disease-free source.
- Get a suitable variety.

DON'T

- Plant in a cold, badly drained site.
- Plant in shallow soil.
- Plant in a heavy soil.
- Plant in the shade of trees or shrubs.
- Plant too deeply.
- Plant diseased runners.
- Plant too close together.

TREE FRUITS

TREES

Many gardens do not have room for large fruit trees, but in the past decade or so apple trees have been miniaturised, making it possible to grow them in smaller spaces, even in containers, and also offering the enticing opportunity of having several varieties on one stem – a kind of mini orchard. Still, the desire of most people is to have larger quantities as well as greater variety, and only bigger trees offer this. Bear in mind that apple, pear and plum trees are permanent features and get bigger and higher every year – even dwarf ones grow, though at a slower rate. Crops grown under the 'rain drip area' of a tree will not succeed as the tress grow big and the trees themselves are also impaired because of competition. Plums are harder to grow than apples, and pears are harder still.

Other tree fruits: There are many more tree fruits that can be grown in Ireland, but they are a bit fussy regarding soil and site, and weather at blossom time. Peaches, nectarines and cherries are occasionally grown, so are apricots and figs. I would consider these beyond the scope of this book.

APPLES

Apple trees can be grown in quite a small area of the garden and are easy enough to grow, with a few basic rules to follow. Like all other crops, they are subject to diseases and pests, have preferences for certain soils and must have shelter. All situations and soils can be improved and not all varieties or rootstocks react in the same way to adverse soil or weather conditions. They hate poor drainage and shallow soils and heavy, wet soils will soon take their toll with canker, while frost hollows will destroy setting blossom year after year.

Apple rootstocks: an apple tree consists of the root portion (a form of crab) onto which a bud from a known variety of apples is grafted. This budding or grafting is done by a skilled budder in spring and so a new apple tree is created. This rootstock controls the growth, the root activity, the ultimate size and cropping habit of the tree, as well as how early in its life it will crop.

There are numerous rootstocks in common use. Vigorous or semi-vigorous trees require large areas to grow and wide spacing (8–10 metres) while the dwarf types can be planted as close as 1 metre apart. Big apple trees produce big crops and small trees produce small crops. The size of the apples will be the same. More than one variety can be grown on one tree and this applies to big as well as small trees. The most important stocks, and their characteristics, are the following:

> M 27 very dwarfing
> M 9 dwarfing
> M 26 semi-dwarfing
> MM 106 semi-vigorous
> MM 111 vigorous
> M 25 very vigorous.

POLLINATION

Basic rules for pollination:

- An apple tree will not and cannot bear fruit without blossom.
- In order to bear blossom, the tree must either be self-fertile

(not needing another tree to pollinate it) or have another apple tree to pollinate it. This other tree must be compatible with it *and* must blossom at the same time (for example, you could buy a Bramley and have a Worcester Pearmain to pollinate it; but you also need a pollinator to pollinate the Worcester Pearmain, and that could be a Laxton Superb). Ornamental crab trees will also do this job. There may be such a tree in a neighbouring garden – it's worth checking this out.

- Bees and other insects carry out the pollination.
- If no blossom is produced, this may be caused by too much vigour, incorrect manure balance (too much nitrogen); there will be no fruit.
- If there is blossom but the majority of the tiny fruit drops off, this may be caused by frost, pests, diseases or drought.

BEST VARIETIES – This is just a short list of what is available.

Cookers

Bramley Seedling is the best-known cooker of all and is a reliable and heavy cropper. It is sterile and needs another variety to pollinate it, which must flower at the same time. Worcester Pearmain makes an excellent pollinator and while it is partially self-fertile it produces better fruit when pollinated by another variety.

Lane's Prince Albert: a small tree, big, juicy apple; reliable cropper; never makes a large tree.

Lord Derby: main crop, good clear skin, disease-free, healthy tree.

Early Victoria (Sheep's Snout): a very early cooker; grows easily but a poor keeper.

Eaters

Beauty of Bath: an early eater, irregular cropper.

Gladstone: an old favourite; early but reliable.

Worcester Pearmain: a good pollinator for Bramley; reliable.

Golden Delicious: green-yellow in colour; reasonable flavour.

Cox's Orange Pippin: best reputation of any apple, but does not do well in Ireland.

Kerry Pippin: a small, yellowish fruit; irregular cropper.

Lord Lambourne: good yellow to red-skinned variety for late cropping in September/October.

Merton Worcester: a second-early variety (September).

Discovery: a September/October variety, with fairly firm flesh.

Idared: very reliable cropper and good storage flavour.

Katja: good colour and flavour; late cropper and good keeper.

James Grieve: excellent flavour and reliable; September/October crop.

Elstar Late: good colour and flavour; October crop.

Jonagold: yellowish-red; good for late October; sterile variety (needs pollinator), stores well.

Charles Ross: large apple; very resistant to scab; rather dry to eat.

How to select a variety:

- First, decide on the space you wish to give to the tree; decide on an eater or a cooker; check out flavour, seasonality, keeping quality, resistance to pests and diseases, reliability of cropping.

- Specific varieties on a specific rootstock can be ordered, usually in early autumn (eg you could order a Charles Ross as a dwarfed variety).
- Apple trees can be purchased from Seed Savers, at Scariff, Co. Clare, especially for old varieties, or from any good garden centre, or ordered by post from specialist nurseries (see Appendix).

HOW TO GROW

Plants

You are planting miniature trees at their baby stage.

Best time to plant: between November and April. Do not plant in frosty, snowy, or very wet conditions, especially if the soil is wet after prolonged rain; if planting in a container (also outdoors), plant at any time of the year.

Best soil: deep, friable, well-drained loam.

Best aspect: the ideal aspect is southerly, but any site between south-east and west will grow a reasonable crop. Choose a gentle slope rather than a flat, level site, so that cold air moves away from the site, especially at blossom time.

Lifespan of trees: up to 40–50 years.

Space per tree: *dwarf variety* 1 metre (39in); *large tree* 8–10 metres (27-30 feet).

Growing situations: open garden; dwarf types can be grown in raised beds or containers. Do not plant in ground where apple trees were grown previously as apple trees suffer from replant disease (they pick up diseases of the previous trees).

Soils and drainage: apple trees will grow in a wide range of soils, but grow best in a medium loam overlying a well-drained subsoil. Where drainage is a problem, whether seasonal or intermittent, this should be improved before apple trees are planted. *Apple canker* (a fungal disease that affects the young and old wood) is always a problem in badly drained soils.

Soil and site preparation: as apples are a longterm crop and will occupy the site for up to 30 or 40 years, it is worthwhile paying attention to the basic requirements:

• Get rid of perennial weeds.

• Make stock-proof by putting up fences to exclude cattle, sheep and horses.

• Keep rabbits out with wire netting.

• Ensure that the soil is not lacking in major nutrients, including lime (soil test). Add lime if pH is below 5.5.

• The ground for apple trees should not be treated with manure, but a dressing of compost is beneficial; mix it well with the soil. Small quantities of moss peat may be added before planting, about ¼ to ¾ soil, and should be mixed well with the soil.

• All perennial weeds such as scutch grass, nettles, thistles, docks, bindweed (convolvolus) and buttercups should be dug out.

STAKING

Apple trees need to be staked, especially the dwarf types, as they have a poor rooting system and can easily be blown over or loosened in the soil. The stake should be 5cm (2in) diameter (or, if square, 5cm x 5cm [2in x 2in]); the height depends on the height of the tree. Drive it into position *before* the tree is planted so as to avoid damage to the roots. Tie the tree to the stake with a rubber or plastic tie that can be adjusted annually.

SHELTER

A windbreak, either natural or artificial, is essential to protect blossoms, to encourage pollinating insects and prevent damage from autumn gales to the ripening fruit. The purpose of a shelter belt is to slow down the speed of the wind by causing it to filter through the windbreak.

MANAGEMENT

Fairly simple pruning, feeding and weed control.

• **Pruning**: the pruning can be divided into two phases: (1) the formation and shaping of the tree, (2) to encourage cropping in an orderly fashion.

(1) The formation of the tree starts off at the nursery (where tree is propagated) and consists of cutting back the shoot that grew in the current year to half or one-third its length. This results in two or more shoots sprouting out the following year. In turn, these two shoots are cut back the following autumn. The ultimate aim is to shape the tree to be open-centred with branches arranged like the ribs of an umbrella. This shape allows light and air into all parts of the tree and gives better ventilation, thus ensuring less disease in fruit and better ripening.

(2) In subsequent years the shoots are cut back each year in autumn or winter, but always before growth starts in spring. Cut out all dead and diseased wood, and any branches that

are crossing each other or crossing into the centre.

- **Note**: a pruned apple tree will crop later in its life than an un-pruned one, but the pruned and managed tree will crop and grow for many years longer.

- **Damage by pets**: cats or rabbits can claw at the trunks of the trees and this can lead to canker or other problems, especially in young trees. As a protection, put a cylinder of plastic (eg plastic piping, rigid netting) around the stem at planting time.

PESTS AND DISEASES

Pests: *Aphids* and *Red Spider* are the chief pests attacking apple trees, but are not serious enough to need control measures.

Diseases: The major disease that attacks apple trees is *apple canker*. This can be reduced by ensuring that soil nutrient levels are in balance, with more potassium (more seaweed feed or wood ash) and less nitrogen (less nettle feed) than other plants, while ensuring that drainage is good. The most serious disease of the fruit is *apple scab* and weather has a huge bearing on its occurrence; there's very little you can do about it, except to select resistant varieties.

HARVESTING

Expect first crop: first year from dwarf types; 2–4 years from others.

When to pick: apples are picked when they are ripe. Apples are ripe when they are easy to pick from the tree, or some have fallen to the ground already.

Storing: store in a dry, cool place that is rat-proof. Never store damaged or diseased fruit and never store early-maturing varieties with or near the longterm varieties. Apples may be individually wrapped in newspapers and this prevents rot spreading from one to another. Handle apples carefully, ensuring they are not squeezed or bruised or let drop.

Good points: Small trees for small gardens. Good range of varieties. Rootstock controls tree size and cropping pattern.

Bad points: Takes a long time to crop. Crop depends on many variables. Small trees give small crops. Takes a lot of space and no other crops can grow under the trees after the first two years.

DO

- Plant in a frost-free site.
- Plant in a sunny position.
- Choose a free-draining soil.
- Select a suitable variety.
- Select the correct rootstock.

DON'T

- Plant in poorly drained soil.
- Plant in exposed situation.
- Plant in poor, shallow soil.
- Plant in weed-infested ground.
- Plant in ground that grew apple trees previously.

PEARS

Pears are harder to grow than apples and do not have the range of rootstocks that are available for apple trees. They are best grown against a wall in a sheltered, southerly aspect. They have similar requirements to apples and the instructions given above should be applied to pears. Like apple trees, they can be purchased from Seed Savers or nurseries or garden centres. Many pear trees are available in vigorous and semi-dwarf rootstock. They take longer than apples to start cropping, usually 3–4 years, they can have a lifespan of up to 50 years or more. I have known several trees that have lived and cropped for over a hundred years. Pear trees are pruned in a similar way to apple trees.

HOW TO GROW

Follow the instructions above for apple trees.

Season for planting: November to April.

Best soil: deep, well-drained, medium loam, similar to apples.

Best aspect: a sheltered southerly aspect.

Best varieties: Conference – very juicy fruit, spreading tree; Doyenne du Comice – great flavour, spreading tree; Buerre Hardy – good flavour, self-fertile.

MANAGEMENT

- As for apples.

PESTS AND DISEASES

Pests: as for apples.

Diseases: *Pear canker*, which is similar to *apple canker*, can be caused by poor drainage and an imbalance in the nitrogen/potassium ratio. Too much nitrogen encourages canker.

HARVESTING

Not all pears ripen on the trees. At the start of leaf fall in September/October, pick off the fruits and store indoors in a dry, cool area and allow to ripen. The pears are ripe when the stem end feels soft to pressure from the thumb. Some varieties will ripen within a week of picking, while others may take much longer, up to two months.

Good points: Good crops possible. Fairly disease-free. Easy management.

Bad points: Not as hardy as apples. Slow to produce initial crop. Tends to grow rather tall.

DO

- Choose a warm, sunny site, well-sheltered.
- Prepare the soil well before planting.
- Clear all perennial weeds before planting.
- Select a suitable variety.

DON'T

- Plant in a cold, exposed situation.
- Plant in a heavy, badly-drained soil.
- Plant too close to other trees or crops.
- Add dung to the soil.

PLUMS

Plums are the most popular tree fruits after apples, and, though not as hardy as apples, they will grow in most gardens. They are best grown against a south-facing wall. They need shelter, especially in early spring as they blossom very early. The average lifespan is 30–35 years, but can be much longer (or shorter). Like apples and pears, they are available at Seed Savers or any garden centre.

HOW TO GROW

The planting, shelter, and pruning is the same as for apples and pears above. The manuring is different, however, in that plums like a rich soil, especially nitrogen, thus lots of manure.

Best season to plant: November to April.
Best soil: deep, well-drained, medium loam.
Best site: well-sheltered site, facing south. Best to grow on a south-facing wall. Can grow in a raised bed.
Eventual size of tree: 4.5–6 metres (15–18ft) tall.
Best variety: Victoria is the best, but is, unfortunately, subject to *silver leaf,* a fatal disease for plums.

MANAGEMENT

Staking, manuring and weed control are all essential.
Best pruning time: August/September.

PESTS AND DISEASES

Pests: *Bullfinches* are serious destroyers of fruit buds in plums during the winter. *Aphids* damage the leaves in the summer and *wasps* can do serious damage to the ripening fruits – put out a jamjar half-full of water, with a little bit of jam smeared on the top and a small entrance hole in the lid.

HARVESTING

Time between planting and first fruit: 2 years.

Good points: Fairly easy to grow. Reliable croppers. No need of pollinator if Victoria is planted.

Bad points: Subject to frost damage. Subject to bud damage by birds.

DO

- Plant in a sheltered situation.
- Plant in a good, fertile soil.
- Plant between November and April.
- Plant in a deep, well-drained soil.
- Plant against a wall or fence.
- Feed liberally.

DON'T

- Plant in exposed situations.
- Plant in poorly drained soils.
- Plant in weedy ground.
- Neglect pruning.

THINGS YOU MAY
NEED TO KNOW

Growing in the Ground and Elsewhere

In the garden you can grow on flat ground or in drills. Drills are ridges where the plant is to grow. There is no difference in yields or crop quality.

FLAT

- Growing on the flat is best for free-draining soils and easier to prepare.

DRILLS

- Growing on drills is harder work than on the flat, but desirable for wet, poorly drained soils.
- Crops grown on drills are easier to keep free of weeds by using a hoe.
- Drills are an essential part of growing potatoes as the soil is put up around the stalks as they grow.

DIGGING THE GARDEN

- Digging should be done as long as possible before planting or seeding. The old custom of digging in autumn and also in winter, and allowing the soil to remain in a rough state over the early spring is good practice. The exposure to the frosts and wind helps to make the preparations easier in spring.
- Some people cover the dug ground with plastic until it's time for planting. This has the advantage of stopping weeds (apart from perennials); ensure you use porous plastic to allow air and moisture through. However, when soil is not covered, frost can kill many of the harmful insects and weeds and also help break down the soil. So there are advantages to each approach.

- Always have a piece of ground dug and ready for sowing seeds because in the Irish climate the number of days suitable for sowing in spring can sometimes be extremely limited.

SPADE OR FORK?

It all depends on the type of soil and weeds present.

- A *spade* is very useful for a soil that has a network of weed roots where each sod can be cut to size and lifted forward.
- A *fork* can then be used to break up the sod and separate the soil from the weeds.
- In less weed-infested areas, a fork can be used directly and the soil lumps broken up, and clods and large stones removed.
- With a little bit of practice it will be possible to pick out the roots of the weeds using a tine of the fork. The weeds are left on top of the soil to be collected and raked off afterwards and put on the compost heap.
- *What type of spade/fork?*
- Get a long, straight handle. A short handle, no matter how fancy, is back-breaking.
- Don't get a spade or fork that is very wide as you will not make as much progress owing to the heavier weight of soil being lifted. A narrow spade will help you to make more progress, with less back-ache.
- A spade should be sharp, and a well used spade is self-sharpening. Clean after use to prevent rust.

DIGGING AND SOIL TEMPERATURE

In mid-winter the coldest soil is on the top and soil gets gradually warmer down to a depth of 15–18cm (6–7in), where it drops to about 3°–4°C. In spring, as the days lengthen, the soil temperature at the surface rises to 5°–6°C, or higher at times. This is the minimum temperature for growth and germination to take place. If cold soil is dug up from a depth of 25–30cm (10–12in), this is going to delay germination and growth.

- Always have soil dug beforehand so that it gets a chance to heat up.
- When soil temperatures rise, weeds begin to grow and this indicates that the soil is ready/almost ready for planting.

RAISED BEDS

A raised bed is a structure like a box or tank containing soil that is raised above ground level for ease of management. The bed can be any shape or size, single-sided (operated from one side only) or double-sided (reached from both sides).

- The height can vary from just 10–12cm (4–5in) to 90cm (3ft).
- They can vary in width from 60–90cm (2–3ft) for a single, to 150–180cm (5–6ft) for a double. Ensure all parts can be reached.
- They can be of any length.
- There should be direct contact between the ground and the soil in the raised bed. A raised bed is different to a container garden where the latter has no direct contact with the soil under it.
- The sides of the bed can be made of concrete, bricks, metal, plastic, wood or old railway sleepers.
- Any crop that can be grown in the open garden can be grown in a raised bed. Very tall crops, such as peas and beans or apple trees, will be slightly beyond reach if grown in raised beds, but for these crops a bed of 30–60cm (1–2ft) height may be sufficient.

Advantages
- It is easier to dig, cultivate, sow seed, manage and harvest because

there is less bending down.

- It is easier to observe the progress of the crops, and pests and diseases are easier to spot and to control.

- They are neat and are well-defined.

- They are usually more productive because they tend to get better attention.

- The soil is warmer because it's drier, being above the level of the surrounding soil.

Disadvantage
- Raised beds dry out much faster than ordinary garden soil.

Filling a Raised Bed
- The bottom layer should always be made of free-draining rubble or stones, and the remainder of good topsoil or compost.

- At least 45cm (18in) of soil is needed – better if it is 60cm (2ft).

- It takes nearly a year for the soil to settle fully and the soil level will drop by as much as 7–10cm (3–4in).

Managing a Raised Bed
- During periods of dry weather, water it regularly when crops are developing. Usually if the top of the bed is dry, then the lower parts will soon be dry also.

- All or a portion of a raised bed can be covered with glass or plastic and this will help to get earlier crops in the spring and later crops in the autumn.

*REMEMBER!

- **Rotation is just as important in a raised bed as in the garden soil (see p258).**

GROWING UNDER PROTECTION

Glasshouse/Polytunnel

- A glasshouse or polytunnel will give an extra month's growth in the spring and another extra month in the autumn.

- They provide a place to work in cold and wet weather, and a place where seeds can be sown in trays for planting out later.

- Many crops can be sown *and* matured there – lettuce, carrots, spring onions, beans, peas, cauliflower, celery, potatoes, strawberries and raspberries are the most popular.

- Temperatures are more even in a glasshouse than in a polytunnel and the glasshouse is more durable.

- A polytunnel is far cheaper to buy and erect, but has to be re-clad after 4–5 years. You can extend this by buying the best quality materials and by protecting the plastic from any rough edges on the framework.

- The best location for a glasshouse is on a south-facing wall or slope. A polytunnel should ideally run on a slope north/south. Shelter is important, but too much shelter can cause shading and loss of sunlight.

- Space within these structures is usually at a premium and priority should be given to those crops that cannot be grown outside at that time. Seeds can be germinated and grown-on there before hardening-off and being transplanted outside. It makes good sense to grow some 'very' early crops of potatoes, carrots, lettuce, onions as well as parsley and strawberries there, and, during the summer, crops like lettuce, tomatoes, cucumbers, melons, aubergines and peppers. Amongst the crops that can be started off in a glasshouse or polytunnel are peas, beans, cauliflower, broccoli, brussels sprouts, sweetcorn, courgettes and parsley.

A Cold Frame

- A cold frame is a structure usually made of concrete, brick or wood, and covered with a glass or plastic frame that can be opened easily – you need to be able to keep it open for a certain period and usually closed at night. It is usually a few centimetres above ground level, which helps drainage, and facing south. It is the next best thing to a glasshouse.

A Hotbed

- A traditional hotbed is composed of a large heap of rotting manure (usually horse/stable manure) on which a glass frame is placed on top of planks of wood (a kind of cold frame). Seeds are sown in pots or seed trays, placed under the frame, and the rotting manure generates heat which helps seeds to germinate and plants to grow. If you have easy access to stable manure, this can be good practice.
- The modern hotbed is made up of electric soil-heating wires going through the soil, or a heating mat, and seed trays are placed over them.

Sun Lounge or Porch

- Fruit and vegetables can be grown in a porch or sun lounge, but the temperature may fluctuate too much and there may not be sufficient light at all times. The porch or sun lounge is better for some crops than the outdoors, but not as good as a glasshouse.

Other Forms of Protection

- The simplest form of protection for plants is jamjars placed over individual plants to give protection and trap heat.
- A cloche is a wire structure with panes of glass (approx. 30–45cm high) with sides and sloping top, somewhat in the shape of a mini shed; polythene cloches are sheets of polythene stretched over wire

hoops inserted in the ground. They are neither waterproof nor air-tight, but they help the covered crop to grow better by keeping out the cold winds and trapping the sun's heat. Their big advantage is that they are portable, but their disadvantage is that they are very fragile and easily blown around by wind.

- A belljar is like a glass dome, not often used nowadays.

- Clear plastic mulch, made of very light plastic with small holes. It is secured at the sides with stones or a covering of soil, laid directly over freshly seeded crops and rises with the crop. It allows the rain to go through the holes, but traps the heat of the sun and keeps off the cold winds.

- Grow fleece is made of non-woven opaque material that allows the heat and rain through, but keeps out the cold winds. It is kept in place at the edges with soil or a plank. It can be re-used several times and also has the advantage that it prevents crops being attacked by insects and birds. As the crop grows in height, the fleece rises with it.

CONTAINERS

- Containers are any vessel or container – from a flower pot to a large box or bag – filled with soil or compost in which you can grow crops.

- Containers can be placed indoors or outdoors.

- Unlike raised beds, containers have no direct contact with soil from which to draw water, so they must be watered regularly.

- The container should be durable and at a satisfactory working height.

- A container should be placed in a sheltered situation, and in the sunniest aspect. It should always be placed in a safe situation and should not be put in a position from which it may fall accidentally.

- Ensure it has adequate drainage.
- When filling with soil or compost, keep out perennial weeds.
- The soil should be fertile and in good physical condition.
- Any good medium-loam soil (good topsoil) is suitable. Peat-based potting composts are also quite suitable and have the advantage that they are free of weeds and weed seeds. These composts need to be replenished annually with nutrients.
- Small containers can be moved in and out of the glasshouse or polytunnel as required.

Advantages:
- Growing in containers – bags or boxes or other containers – has the advantage of being in the complete control of the grower. They can be fed and watered at will (but they will dry out) and there is less of a problem with weeds.
- The containers can be mobile and moved into the best position from time to time.
- In winter, the container can be emptied and stored away until spring.

Disadvantages:
- Plants growing in containers are completely dependent on the grower supplying water on a regular basis.
- The number of plants and crops is more limited.

ORGANIC OR NOT?

- This book is aimed at growing organically. I don't use chemicals on my vegetables and fruit. Lack of use of chemicals on food crops may lead to losses when pests attack, but there are controls other than chemicals, which I prefer to use.

- By understanding and working with nature rather than against it, certain pests can be reduced or eliminated entirely. I give suggestions for individual crops based on my own experience.

Best Organic Practices
- The old practice of rotating crops (see p258) so that no two members of the same family follow on the same patch of ground in two or more successive years is as old as agriculture itself. This is sound advice.

- Sowing or planting specific crops at earlier or later dates can also help to reduce losses. I have given guidelines for best dates for each crop.

- The need for good soil preparation will also go a long way to achieving success. Many soils may not be ideal for growing and will need humus or organic matter to be added before crops can thrive.

- Providing good climatic growing conditions is as important as soil conditions.

- Constant monitoring is necessary to ensure that your efforts are not brought to nought by an attack from slugs, birds, disease or pests.

Pluses and Minuses of Organic Growing
- All chemicals have some effect on health, mostly an adverse one. Most people now believe that everybody's health is better without the use of chemicals and without a constant build-up by over-use of them over years. We want our food to be chemical-free, as far as possible.

- Home-produced garden compost is used by organic growers. Along with supplying some or all of the nutrients that plants need, it also supplies humus (organic matter), which helps to improve the physical condition of the soil. (It also recycles a lot of household waste.)

- Good crops can be grown without chemicals, but it is possible to get better-looking and larger vegetables and fruits by using chemicals.

- Organic growing is more difficult and demanding, and yields of organic crops are generally well below those of crops grown using chemicals. Weeds, pests and diseases are harder to control.

- The reward in the end is really worth it as there is the certainty that no chemicals have been used and so you are more in control of your health. The flavour and texture of your crops, as well as their colour, are usually far better.

USE OF CHEMICAL FERTILISERS

If you are going organic, then the following basic information about chemical additions to soil is of no interest to you. I include it, however, for those who wish to use it, though I do not give specific instructions for use with each crop. It is essential to follow the instructions given with a chemical fertiliser. Chemical fertilisers are highly specific and should not be messed around with.

- Artificial fertilisers supply one or more of the major elements to the growing plant. A typical example is 10:10:20: the first 10 stands for the nitrogen (N) percentage content, the second 10 stands for the phosphate percentage content and the 20 stands for the percentage content of potassium. Nitrogen helps leaf growth, phosphates help in the development of roots, seeds and fruit, potassium helps build up resistance to diseases and helps to develop flavour. These artificial fertilisers offer a readily available supply of plant food within easy reach of the plant.

CROP ROTATION

- It is good practice to rotate crops.

Reasons

- Different crops have different needs and attract different pests and diseases. If the same crops are grown in the same plot of ground year after year, then the same amount and type of nutrients are drawn off each year, and the number of pests and diseases will increase hugely.

- Though many pests are common to a lot of crops, there are some that are specific to a particular crop. To prevent a build-up of a particular pest, a crop is grown in a different plot every year over several years before it comes back again to the original plot. In this way, any residues of the original crop, together with any relevant pests and diseases, will have all but disappeared after an absence of a few years. The longer the break, the better; many people work to a four-year cycle, which is what I'd advise, ideally, and have followed in my instructions above. Even a one-year break is better than no break.

- Some crops, such as potatoes and cabbages, like an addition of manure or compost, while others, like carrots and parsnips, prefer not to get manure or compost as it causes forking of the roots.

- Potatoes, because there is usually a bigger amount of them grown in the plot, are usually allocated one place in the rotation for themselves. Other areas contain mixed crops.

- The members of the cabbage family, called brassicas, comprising cabbages, kale, cauliflower, brussels sprouts, broccoli, radish, turnips, swedes and kohl rabi are treated as another separate group. They are subject to a disease variously called *gout, finger and toe,* or *club root* and these names are descriptive of the appearance of the roots. This disease remains in the ground for many years and when a suscepti-ble crop is planted it picks up the disease on the new roots. There is no known cure for it. Therefore brassicas must move around and not return to the same growing spot for at least three to four years.

Plan of Rotation
- The plot may be divided into four or five areas. Use *five* if you plan on having a permanent plot of rhubarb, asparagus, strawberries, herbs or artichokes (they remain outside the rotation). This plot can be brought into use for other crops if disease has gained the upper hand. The remaining four are usually allocated as follows:

YEAR ONE
- **AREA 1** potatoes, **AREA 2** brassicas, **AREA 3** roots, **AREA 4** 'others'.
- Roots are made up of carrots, parsnips, beetroot.
- 'Others' include peas, beans, celery, celeriac, onions, leeks, marrows, courgettes, lettuce, sweetcorn.

YEAR TWO
- **AREA 1** brassicas; **AREA 2** roots; **AREA 3** 'others', **AREA 4** potatoes.

YEAR THREE
- **AREA 1** roots; **AREA 2** 'others'; **AREA 3** potatoes, **AREA 4** brassicas.

YEAR FOUR
- **AREA 1** 'others'; **AREA 2** potatoes; **AREA 3** brassicas, **AREA 4** roots.

Rules:

- Give dung or compost to the potatoes, brassicas and 'others'.
- Do NOT give dung to the root crops.
- Rotation rules, of course, do not follow a calendar year. There is a certain amount of overlapping, for example, spring cabbage is sown in July but not harvested until the following March or April. Where do you sow it? You sow it in the brassica plot for the coming year. It is not possible always to stick to the calendar, but be aware always of the dangers of diseases and do not be tempted to continue to use the same plot for a particular crop any two years in a row, no matter how good it has been in a previous year.
- **Inter-cropping**: means growing a fast-maturing crop in between two rows of a slower-growing crops that are planted widely apart. Examples would be growing lettuce or radish in between rows of raspberries or rhubarb. This can be combined with the rotation plan.

Families of Vegetables

The brassica family: the biggest group, with cabbage, cauliflower, brussels sprouts, kale, broccoli, kohl rabi, turnips, swedes and radishes.

The solanaceae family: potatoes, tomatoes, aubergines and peppers.

The legume family: comprise all the beans and peas.

The umbelliferae family: carrots, parsnips, parsley, celery, celeriac, fennel and dill.

The allium family: onions, leeks and chives.

The chenopodiaceae family: is represented by beetroot, Swiss chard and spinach.

The cucurbitaceae family: vegetable marrow, courgette, cucumber, pumpkin, melon and gherkin.

The compositae family: globe and Jerusalem artichokes, chickory, endive, lettuce and salsify.

Basic Things – improving your garden

ASPECT

- While many other factors about a garden can be changed, the aspect is fixed. As Ireland lies in the northern hemisphere, a southerly aspect is always the warmest and a definite advantage for any crop for earliness or number of growing days.

- A northerly aspect is the coldest and gives the least number of growing days per year, and is the last to start growing in the spring.

- Westerly and easterly aspects are intermediate in taking advantage from the heat of the sun, the former getting the advantage in the afternoon and the latter in the forenoon. The easterly position has the disadvantage of getting the cold, easterly winds that our forebears dreaded (they depended totally on their vegetable plots), and still cause a lot of crop damage.

- A bad aspect cannot be improved, but all the other factors such as shelter, soil fertility, drainage should be at their best to compensate for this lack. A bad aspect will limit the range of crops that can be grown in a garden.

SLOPE

- A very gentle slope to the south is ideal – it attracts most light.

- A level plot is easier to work, move equipment and compost around, as well as being easier to hoe.

- A steep slope is a disadvantage and harder to work. You could terrace it, but this is an expensive exercise and needs to be done by a competent engineer. The retaining walls must be properly built to withstand the force of weight. Make sure to remove the topsoil first and replace it when the terracing has been completed.

SHELTER

- Shelter is important for most crops and nearly every site in Ireland benefits from some shelter from wind, whether in the form of a natural shelter belt (trees, a hedge) or an artificial barrier.

- Shelter raises the temperature of the site, promotes earlier growth and increases the number of growing days, so it helps to produce bigger crops, earlier crops and promotes earlier ripening of fruit.

- Plant a shelter belt of trees or a hedge along the windswept boundary, or erect an artificial barrier (wood, plastic or metal) to reduce the force of the wind.

- A semi-permeable shelter is better than a solid one as it allows the wind to filter through rather than bouncing over it and causing turbulence.

- For every unit in height, a barrier gives shelter or wind-speed reduction of ten times that in length. So a 150cm (5ft) high barrier gives shelter extending to 15m (50ft) on the leeward side.

- Shelter provides a warmer micro-climate, allowing pollinating insects to work earlier and longer hours.

- There is less damage done to plants being blown around. Fruit is not blown off trees and bushes.

*BEWARE!

- **A garden can be over-sheltered to the detriment of plants. It can have so many trees that there is very little light, except in mid-summer.**

- **If shelter blocks the movement of air, diseases and pests can become established and will be very hard to eradicate.**

- **Also, soil dries badly in an enclosed, poorly ventilated garden.**

- **The rain drip from foliage is sometimes sufficient to extend humid conditions and spark off an outbreak of disease.**
- **Roots of trees and hedges invade ground space quite a lot and will encroach on areas intended for fruit and vegetables. Large and fast-growing trees will extend out for more than 3–4m (10–12ft) and will interfere with digging and cultivation and compete for water and nutrients. Hedges will do the same, but to a lesser extent.**

COLD GARDENS

- A north-facing garden has a later and shorter growing season. Cold gardens get off to a much later start in the spring.
- Shelter should be provided and full use should be made of growing aids such as glasshouses, polytunnels, cloches, cold frames.
- The northerly aspect limits the range, the quality and yields you can achieve.
- The only positive side to cold gardens is that they are less prone to a lot of the insects normally associated with warm gardens.

PATHS

- Paths make for clear divisions between plots.
- They are easier to keep than grassed areas and more defined.
- Weeds and stones can be placed on the paths while preparing seedbeds.
- It is easier to wheel a wheelbarrow on a firm path rather than on grass or soil.

A NEW OR NEGLECTED GARDEN
New garden

- In a new garden (if you have a choice), look for good, deep, well-drained, rich soil, a good aspect, preferably south, gentle slope, well sheltered and in a good state of cultivation (free of brambles and perennial weeds). The garden should be well fenced or walled-in.

- After the builder has left it, remove any large lumps of concrete, concrete blocks, bricks, timber off-cuts, broken tiles, plastic sheeting, copper and plastic pipes, and wire cables.

- The whole area needs to be dug over and an assessment made as to whether the soil is good topsoil or not. If there is a doubt, get advice on it and get good topsoil in rather than struggle for years with a substandard material. Be careful of the soil you buy in and be satisfied it *really* is good.

A lawn

- A lawn, even a neglected lawn, can make an excellent fruit or vegetable garden. Over the years there would have been a build-up of humus in the soil. Pests, diseases and weed seeds will be almost completely absent.

Neglected garden

- In an old, neglected garden, the first thing to clear is any briars and woody plants by digging out with a spade.

- Next, any overhanging trees or shrubs will have to be cut back.

- Check that drainage is not impeded.

- Perennial weeds might need to be treated with a weedkiller. This is the one occasion on which I use a chemical weedkiller, glyphosate (eg Roundup), because I feel that this is the only sensible way to deal with permanent weeds such as scutch grass. This particular chemical compound is ultimately broken down by the soil organisms.

- The initial tilling after reclaiming might have to be by spade or garden rotovator if the ground is too rough.

- Neglected gardens can give fantastic results after renewal has taken place, because the years of neglect have allowed for a build-up of humus and fertility, and pests and diseases have usually died out.

BRIARS

- If your site is overrun with briars, cut them back and dig the roots out individually.

- While a heavy machine may be brought in to remove a layer of soil containing the roots and stems, this valuable layer is too precious to tear away and dump. The aim should be to get rid of the briars *without* removing the soil. The task should be done in stages, as it will appear less daunting – and the autumn/winter period is best time to start because there is less growth to get in your way.

GARDEN PLAN

- Every garden should start with a plan; and a plan should be made each year.

- This ensures crop rotations are followed.

- It ensures the garden is utilised more efficiently.

- Manure and compost are applied where required.

- Projections for the year should be included as well as present position.

- A simple diagram, showing where crops will be, is essential.

- Draw up the plan in the winter or early spring.

- Stick to the plan – but it must also be flexible, as unexpected weather and other surprises can call for a need to change.

- Past records are very useful in drawing up a plan.

- Evaluate the plan at the end of the year.

- Record the seasonal progress in a diary or notebook.

What to put in your garden plan

- Start off by making a list of the crops you would like to grow. Make a priority list, then make a list of the order of sowing.

- Then decide on the varieties of each vegetable you wish to grow. These varieties could be decided on with the help of this book, information from other plot holders or your own previous experience. You might also like to experiment!

- Decide where you will plant each crop, following your rotation scheme.

- Mark the spots where you need to dig-in manure or compost.

SOIL

THE BEST SOIL

- Deep, friable or crumbly loam, well drained, dark brown/black colour, that is easy to dig. The physical quality of the soil is as important, or more so, than the nutrient content. Soils of a light brown colour usually indicate low content of humus and are poor as well as being difficult too work. If the soil colour is light to dark brown and has a good texture, then the humus content can be built up over the years. Beware of buying in soil that has a poor colour.

- The soil is a living thing and contains many living organisms that interact with each other and with the crops that are growing in it. The soil itself is made up of stones of varying sizes, sand, clay, silt, insects, bacteria, fungi, viruses, remains of plants and animals and numerous weed seeds. There is constant change taking place and the mere task of digging aids this change.

- Natural plant food is derived from clay particles and stones,

THINGS YOU MAY NEED TO KNOW

decaying plant material (humus) in the form of compost and nitrogen from the atmosphere.

- Good soils that have perennial weeds, such as scutch grass or nettles, are worthwhile as these can be cleared off and the good soil remains.

- A very sandy soil, while easy to work and which produces early crops, is not the best, but can be improved over the years by the addition of dung or compost.

SOIL IN CONTAINERS

- There are very few sources of good topsoil. The more likely places are where new roads or buildings are starting – it is best to find local supplies as the cost of transportation can make the cost of topsoil prohibitive. Good topsoil that is being cleared from a site is suitable, provided it does not contain too much subsoil or large stones.

- If you need to buy-in soil, a soil-based or John Innes-type compost is suitable.

BAD SOIL

- Poor weed growth, difficult to dig, slow to drain, spongy to walk on, poor colour – grey, light-brown or yellow.

- If there is water on the soil and moss is present, this shows that the soil is not good for growing. Moss and other plants do not do well together.

- Heavy, wet soils.

- Very exposed soils at high elevations.

- Very shallow, stony soils are unsuitable for most crops and cannot be improved easily.

SANDY SOIL

- Easy to work, dig and rake and is usually very free-draining. Work can commence much earlier in the year and last longer in the autumn.

- Produces earlier crops.

- Poor in nutrients as they are easily washed out. Sandy soils are usually hungry.

- In dry weather, crops will come under stress for want of water much earlier than in loamy soils.

STONES

- Stones help drainage and keep a soil open and porous.

- Stones in various sizes and shapes and different composition are the source of many of the minerals that become available to plants.

- Rake-off the large stones – those over 5–7cm (2–3in) in diameter – near the surface and either dispose of them by burying them down deeper, or put them to one side, or use them to make an informal path between different sections of the garden. Better still, use them as a soak-way in the lowest part of the garden – dig a hole and put them into it, and cover with soil. Leave the small stones – if all stones are raked off, the soil is easily compacted and provides a very poor growth medium.

- The concrete, stone or brick debris left behind by a builder can be buried in a hole to help drainage, but do not bury pieces of plastic or wood – the former can impede drainage and the latter drains the soil of nutrients, especially nitrogen, as it rots down over the years.

IMPROVING THE SOIL

- The physical condition of soil can be improved by the addition of animal manures, compost, moss peat or green manuring (sowing a crop and digging it in, see p275).

- Animal manures and compost, along with improving the soil physically, will also improve the nutrient status. This material must be incorporated into the soil by digging or by rotovating.

- A heavy, wet soil can be improved by the addition of organic material and ensuring that drainage is not impeded (it might need to be drained and this entails laying a land-drain pipe or make a channel from the highest to the lowest part of the land, leading to a soak-away area).

- Organic material may take several years and many applications to achieve the right results, but the more crops that are grown there the better the soil becomes. Where a soil starts off with a low level of nutrients, it takes a number of seasons before the fertility is built up and crops may not give of their best in the first year of tilling.

- If the soil has a moderately high level of nutrition, then the annual addition of compost is simply replacing what the crop is removing. If nutrients are not replaced as crops take them up from the soil, then the soil becomes poor and may not grow certain crops or may produce poor yields.

- The plant determines what it is going to take up from the soil and the nutrients must be in solution in the soil water before this can happen. If there is a shortage or total absence of a major or minor element in the soil, the plant will either fail completely or display symptoms such as stunting, yellowing of leaves, premature seeding or some other sign. (Some of these symptoms might also denote a pest or disease present or the result of extreme weather conditions.)

- A warm soil is needed for growth. A southerly aspect is better than a northerly one, a sheltered site is better than an exposed one, a water-retaining or heavy soil is colder than a sandy, free-draining soil. A dark, black soil absorbs and holds heat much better than a light or dark brown type. A sandy soil heats up faster and can produce earlier crops than a dark clay soil.

TESTING

***TESTING THE SOIL STRUCTURE

- **Take a fistful of wet soil and let it drop from a height of 60cm (2ft) from the ground. If the lump stays intact, it is of poor structure, but if it breaks into small crumbs, then it is good.**

***TESTING THE SOIL FOR NUTRIENTS

- **A simple test kit for pH (acidity or alkalinity) and major nutrients is usually available at garden centres.**
- **If the soil is severely deficient in one of the major elements like phosphates or potassium, then it is as well to know what is needed to get good returns rather than working blindly. You can add extra compost, manure (nitrogen and phosphates) or seaweed (phosphate and potassium).**

***SIMPLE DRAINAGE TEST

- **Dig a hole 30cm cubed (one cubic foot) in volume, 30cm (1ft) deep. If the hole is full after a heavy rainfall, take note of the time it takes to drain away. If it takes more than 24 hours to empty after the end of the rainfall, then drainage is regarded** as poor or impeded. It might be semi-impeded, of course, and take 12 hours to clear. These situations can be addressed by using drills or raised beds.

DON'T

- **Work soil in wet weather as the structure of the soil is damaged if it is dug or cultivated under wet conditions.**

SOIL CONDITIONERS
These help improve the physical condition of soil.

Moss peat:
- Moss peat is good for light soils to make them more retentive of moisture and for heavy soils to make them more open.
- Moss peat should always be mixed well with the soil and preferably be watered in. It has no nutritional value and while plants might survive in moss peat, without soil, for a short time, they will not thrive and will eventually die.
- Never put thick layers of it into a trench.

Wood chippings:
- Use sparingly as these deplete the nitrogen in the soil.

Wood ash:
- I recommend the use of wood ash, but *not* in large quantities as it makes the soil heavy and compact.
- It adds minerals and nutrients, especially potassium.
- Ash from other sources (such as coal, briquettes) may supply trace elements, but has a deleterious effect on the physical condition of the soil and compost heaps.

Seaweed and leaves:
- Old gardeners laid a lot of store on the use of seaweed, which is rich

in many trace elements as well as organic matter. They always allowed it to rot well into the top of the soil before they dug it in. In this way, the harmful effects of the salt are weathered away.

- Leaf mould (compost made from fallen leaves) was another material favoured by gardeners for stretching garden compost.

COMPOST

What is it?

Potting compost: seed or potting compost is sold in bags and contains chemicals.

Garden compost: is from your own garden and is recycled organic materials.

- Garden compost is sweet-smelling, friable, crumbly, dark brown or black material resulting from plant or organic material being left to rot in a compost heap over a period of time. It is really recycled plants. Compost is the next best thing to manure for the garden.

- It can be used as a soil enricher and conditioner before sowing or planting all crops.

How to make garden compost

- Use a container like a large dustbin, with drainage and a cover to keep the rain off. It can also be made in an open heap in a sheltered part of the garden.

- All plant materials, including fruit, vegetables and light woody materials, lawn mowings, hedge trimmings, kitchen waste (excluding meat, fish and cooked materials) can be used. They are allowed to rot down, with the aid of insects, bacteria and viruses over a period of time, usually over a year, or preferably two.

- Do not add chemicals, fertilisers or accelerators.

- Do not add plastic, rubber, metal, heavy wood, paint, oil, grease, fat, cooking oil, meat and meat products.

- Avoid putting in any woody materials or too many grass mowings at any one time. If it does get in, heavy woody materials can be put back in if they have not rotted fully.

- You can include plants damaged by pests, or bolted plants and thinnings.

- Do not use diseased plants, like cabbages that suffered *finger and toe*.

- Wood ash can be added, but make sure that this is well mixed with vegetable materials.

- Put thin layers of material in, keeping a good mix, never a deep layer of any one material like lawn mowings.

- All kinds of insects, including ants, woodlice, beetles, caterpillars, worms, millipedes and centipedes, contribute to the breakdown of the material. Fungi, bacteria and viruses all play their part in the conversion to humus.

- Accelerators (bacterial) are available to speed up the composting process, but I don't use them – I prefer to let it take its time.

- The finished product – humus – should be friable, sweet-smelling and easy to handle.

- Put back any un-rotted material on the compost heap for further rotting.

A smaller version – below ground:
- If you have surplus organic materials and don't wish to make an actual compost heap, then you could simply dig a deep trench in an unused part of the garden, say 45–60cm (18–24in), and put the material there. Organic materials comprise potato stalks, cabbage leaves, rhubarb leaves. They will rot away there and incorporate themselves into the soil as humus.

HUMUS
What is it?

- Humus is the finished product of decomposed plant remains from the compost heap.

- It acts like a sponge; it absorbs water and releases it gradually as the plant roots require it.

- Soil gets richer as humus is added; it becomes darker, more easily worked and less lumpy.

- Humus also releases its own nutrients as the breakdown takes place.

- The soil then has a readily available supply of plant nutrients at its disposal for the nourishment of the growing plant.

More humus – more slugs:

- The downside of adding humus is that the more humus, the more slugs and snails. They form part of the breakdown of the vegetable matter, just like the earthworms and other insects in the soil. You need to be extra vigilant and active in prevention of crop damage.

FARMYARD MANURE

- Farmyard manure supplies the major nutrients, acts as an excellent soil conditioner and often contains minor and trace elements which are vital for plant growth.

- It can vary a lot, depending on the source and method of storage and age – the older the better (if stored under cover).

- It contains less nitrogen, potassium and phosphates than artificial fertilisers.

OTHER ANIMAL MANURES
Horse manure:

- Generally regarded as being better than farmyard manure both in

nutrient value and as a soil conditioner.
- Still fairly accessible and usually free for the taking.
- Store fresh manure in as dry a place as possible – in an open shed or covered with a plastic sheet until it is time to use it, after about a year.

Poultry manure:
- Very high in nitrogen.
- Not the most pleasant material to handle as it is very smelly.
- Should never be used fresh, but left for about 6 months; it is a good idea to mix it with straw or moss peat before storing it in a dry area.

Pig manure:
- Regarded as being too acidic for most vegetable crops and is best spread over the ground over the winter for incorporation during the spring.

GREEN MANURING
- This means growing a crop over the late autumn and winter that can be dug in as the soil is being prepared in spring. The crops usually sown are mustard or white clover, and are sown as soon as the last autumn crop is cleared and soil is tilled over lightly. Seeds are scattered by hand and soil raked over them to cover. Green manuring prevents soil erosion and uses up available nutrients that can be released into the soil again when it is dug in.

LIME
- In the past, a lot of stress was laid on the addition of lime to cope with soil acidity, but very few Irish soils are so low that they might need the addition of lime; most are near neutral (pH 6.5) and this is suitable for most crops.

- Where acidity is suspected, then a small test kit, obtainable at garden centres, will provide the answer.

- Builder's lime or slaked lime can be used, probably a once-off job.

- Ground limestone (calcium carbonate), which is used in agriculture, is available in some garden centres and has the advantage of being beneficial over 5–7 years.

- Spent mushroom compost also has a lot of limestone and is good to neutralise acidity in soils as well as improving the texture of the soil; it's available at many garden centres.

- Lime also supplies calcium.

- High levels of lime will produce scabby potatoes, which as a rule are much drier in texture, while acid soils produce very clean-skinned potatoes.

- Where lime needs to be applied, then always try and put it on a brassica crop, as it has a very positive effect in preventing *club root*.

WEATHER

FROST

- The greatest destroyer of plants in the Irish climate. Frost was a huge issue for Irish growers in former times and I well remember gardeners worrying about it and wondering anxiously when it was safe to plant out the delicate new plants. We seem to get less nowadays, and first frosts are getting later and later; we are also getting better warnings, but as we all know, weather prediction in Ireland is extremely chancy.

- Frost destroys young plants in the early months of the year.

- It often comes as a kind of surprise – just when you think the likelihood of a visit is over, in March for example, it can take your whole crop in one night.

- Early sown crops that become frost-damaged may fail to grow or are erratic in emerging.

- The closer a garden is to sea level the less likely it is to get frost, and even if it does, it will not last as long.

- Frost damage relates to how severe it is as well as the duration – but a short, severe spell is less damaging than a prolonged spell at less severe temperatures. Severity of frost affects emerging or un-hardened-off plants, while a prolonged frost will affect un-harvested mature plants more.

- In autumn, a sudden frost can damage a late maturing vegetable (cauliflower or broccoli). And fruit is sometimes destroyed before it is ready to harvest.

- Certain areas are more subject to frost than others and there can be frost hollows where cold air accumulates and is unable to drain away because of physical barriers. Micro-climates can exist in some districts – it is always best to ask some of the older locals whose livelihoods once depended on knowing about such things. Frost hollows have a shorter growing season and there is very little that can be done to improve the situation.

What you can do

- For earlier-sown crops, use plastic sheets (mulch), fleece or cloches.

- Keep seedlings under cover in glasshouses, polytunnels for longer than standard.

- Be careful of planting-out time – follow the guide given on the seed packet and do not sow before the recommended date – but beware, the Irish climate does *not* follow seed-packet instructions. Have a good look at the weather and check any weather forecasts. If in doubt, wait. And then pray.

RAINFALL AND DRAINAGE

- Rainfall is something over which we have no control, but where the soil is heavy and there is impeded drainage then there are problems for the gardener.
- The solution or improvements lie in correcting the drainage and conditioning the soil by adding in humus or organic matter.
- However, in peaty soil there is a surplus of humus – in that case, stones, sand and gravel should be added.
- Where drainage is a problem the surplus water should be taken from the highest point to the lowest point (soak-pit) using drainage pipes or stones.
- Make sure that any surface water from surrounding areas is not finding its way into the garden, for example from a down-pipe. Raised beds may form the answer to such problems.

WEEDS

PERENNIAL WEEDS

- Like perennial plants, they come back year after year.
- Dig out all the roots and put them on a small, separate compost heap; it may take a while for rotting down to take place and some may even dry out and die.
- Some gardeners spray them with a weed-killer containing Glyphosate, between April and October, in dry weather; after four to five weeks the weeds die back and are removed, complete with roots. I have occasionally done this, but only on areas in which no crops are

grown for about a year.

- Some perennial weeds are harder to get rid of than others, for example bindweed and bishopweed. Annual digging and growing of crops will, however, get rid of most perennial weeds.

ANNUAL WEEDS
- Annual weeds grow from seed every year and will grow rapidly under good weather conditions.
- They compete with the crops for nutrients, water, ground space (roots) and air space (sun).
- The frequent use of a hoe, combined with hand-weeding, is the only way to cope.
- Remove the weeds while they are still small, but not before they can be distinguished from the emerging crop.
- Stop annual weeds going to seed and reproducing.
- Some annual weeds may have more than one generation in the year and these are referred to as 'ephemerals'. An example is groundsel. Keep weeding them out.

BIENNIAL WEEDS
- Biennial weeds germinate and grow in the first year, and in the second year develop a flowering stem and set seeds, for example ragwort and foxglove.

WHAT TO DO ABOUT WEEDS
- A woven plastic mulch sheet laid over the ground and kept down at the edges will keep weeds down while allowing the rainwater to soak through. It is ideal for planting soft fruits and rhubarb – they grow through holes in the plastic.

HOE- AND HAND-WEEDING

- A hoe should be used when seedling weeds appear.

- Use the hoe when the soil is dry. Never hoe in wet soil conditions.

- Hoe to within 2.5cm (1in) of the line of crop seedlings.

- Hand-weed to pluck weeds growing beside and in between the crop plants. The hoe is not accurate enough to clear all the weeds and some of the crop seedlings may be accidentally knocked out or damaged.

WEEDKILLERS

- Not an option for organic growers.

MORE ABOUT WEEDS

- Many of the pests and diseases that attack crops also attack some weeds.

- Weeds are good indicators of soil conditions: nettles indicate good, rich soil, high in humus; thistles and docks indicate deep soil; rushes and reeds indicate poor drainage; red dead nettle and groundsel indicate that soil has been in continuous cultivation for a long time and needs a change in rotation.

- Where weeds thrive is a good indication that vegetable crops will also thrive.

- The toughest weeds are scutch grass, bindweeds (greater and field), bishopweed, creeping sowthistle and creeping buttercup.

- All crops are susceptible to damage from weeds because there is competition for nutrients, moisture and light. Even tall crops like peas and beans are damaged by low weeds because the weed roots are competing for nutrients and moisture.

- Weeds can be put in the compost heap – but not perennials.

APPENDIX

Most seeds and plants are bought at local garden centres or nurseries, but the following brief list of sources may be of help, especially with more unusual plants.

Irish Seed Savers, Capparoe, Scariff, Co. Clare.
Tel. (061) 921866; e-mail: info@irishseedsavers.ie

Brown Envelope Seeds, Ardagh, Church Cross, Skibbereen Co. Cork.
Tel. (028) 38184; e-mail: madsmckeevern@eircom.net; www.brownenvelope-seeds.com

The Herb Garden, Ford-de-Fyne, The Naul, Co. Dublin.
Tel. (01) 8413907; www.the herbgarden.ie

The Organic Centre, Rossinver, Co. Leitrim.
Tel. (072) 54338

Rijk Zwaan De Lier, Holland, via agent Acseed Ltd, David O'Sullivan, Black-rock, Co. Dublin.
Tel. (01) 2803124

Deelish Garden Centre, Ballydehob, Co. Cork,
(agents for Chase Organics Ltd., Hersham, Surrey, KT12 4RG)
Tel. (028) 21374

Europrise, Blake's Cross, Lusk, Co. Dublin,
(agents for Enza Zaden, Holland)
Tel. (01) 8438711

Fruit Hill Farm, Trawlebawn, Bantry, Co. Cork
Tel. (027) 50710; www: fruithillfarm.com

Norma Kenny & Deirdre O'Sullivan, Carbery, Co. Kildare.
E-mail: nurney@eircom.net

SUPPLIERS OF POLYTUNNELS
Colm Warren Polyhouses Ltd., Kilmurray, Trim, Co. Meath.
Tel. 0405 46007; e-mail: deirdrewarren@cwp.ie

Deker Horticulture Supplies Ltd., Tullyard, Trim, Co. Meath.
Tel. 046 31422; e-mail: sales@dekerhort.ie

National Agro Chemicals Distributors Ltd., Blake's Cross, Lusk, Co. Dublin.
Tel. (01) 8427808; e-mail@infodadirl.com

SUPPLIER OF FRUIT TREES AND BUSHES
Patrick English, Raheenduff, Adamstown, Co. Wexford.
Tel. (053) 9240504
Patrick English is the only supplier of tree fruits and soft fruits in Ireland with
such a large range readily available in stock. Most garden centres have a very
limited range of fruit trees and bushes available at any one time, but can
order a specific variety from the UK or Holland.

HAND SEEDERS
Planet Junior: a light, simple, easy-to-push seeder. Discs with different hole
sizes to suit various seeds. Available also in multi units for tractor mounting.
Stanhay: hand-pushed unit or tractor-mounted. Uses a system of holes
punched in a belt that is driven independently of the land wheel. Holes are
punched to accommodate the seed size. Belts are cheap and durable. The
output of seed is regulated by the distance between the holes in the seedbelt.
Webb: hand-pushed or tractor-mounted units. Uses a system of holes in a
rotating cylinder by gears by the land wheel.

TYPICAL N (NITROGEN) P (PHOSPHOROUS) AND K (POTASSIUM) LEVELS
OF ANIMAL MANURES
Cattle slurry: N 3.6 kg per tonne; P 0.6 kg per tonne K 4.3 kg. per tonne
Pig slurry: N 4.6 kg per tonne; P 0.9 kg per tonne; K 2.6 kg. per tonne
Poultry slurry: N 14.2 kg per tonne; P 5.1 kg. per tonne; K 5.7 kg per tonne
Farmyard manure: N 4.6 kg per tonne; P 1.0 kg per tonne; K 6.8 kg per tonne
Seaweed: N 0.1%; K 4% (as potash)

NOTES

NOTES

NOTES

NOTES

NOTES

NOTES